Inflation-Proof Your Portfolio

Inflation-Proof Your Portfolio

HOW TO PROTECT YOUR MONEY
FROM THE COMING
GOVERNMENT HYPERINFLATION

David Voda

WILEY

John Wiley & Sons, Inc.

Published by John Wiley & Sons, Inc., Hoboken, New Jersey.
Published simultaneously in Canada.

For general information on our other products and services or for technical support, please contact our Customer Care Department within the United States at
(800) 762-2974, outside the United States at (317) 572-3993 or fax (317) 572-4002.

Wiley also publishes its books in a variety of electronic formats. Some content that
appears in print may not be available in electronic books. For more information
about Wiley products, visit our web site at www.wiley.com.

Library of Congress Cataloging-in-Publication Data:

Voda, David, 1953-
    Inflation-proof your portfolio : how to protect your money from the coming
government hyperinflation / David Voda.
        p.   cm.
    Includes bibliographical references and index.
    ISBN 978-1-118-24927-7 (cloth); ISBN 978-1-118-28321-9 (ebk);
    ISBN 978-1-118-28437-7 (ebk); ISBN 978-1-118-28632-6 (ebk)
        1. Investments.   2. Portfolio management.   3. Inflation (Finance)
4. Business cycles.   I. Title.
    HG4521.V63   2012
    332.024—dc23

                                                          2012009219

Printed in the United States of America
10 9 8 7 6 5 4 3 2

To Pat Allen

Contents

Principle 2   Future Money Is Cheap Money

Principle 3   Diversify Out of Dollars

Preface

Like you, I'm worried. In the midst of the worst economic crisis since the Great Depression, the politicos in Washington seem intent on driving the country toward bankruptcy. The current administration's 2011 budget is 50 percent higher than it was just three years ago—and National Public Radio reports there will be at least $13 trillion in deficits in the next 10 years.[1,2]

When President Obama was elected to office in January 2009, the national debt totaled $10.626 trillion. Now, in August of 2011, the debt has exploded by another $4 trillion according to CBS News.[3]

"On average," reports Zeke Miller of Businessinsider.com, "the national debt increased $4.247 billion during each day Obama has been in office."[4] By 2020, the nonpartisan Congressional Budget Office projects yet another $8.5 trillion in deficits—creating a national debt that amounts to 90 percent of the entire economy.[5] Over the next decade, the government plans to borrow almost $80,000 for each U.S. household.[6] For every household in America, the government is currently promising to pay future benefits amounting to $212,500 in Medicare, $183,400 in Social Security payments, and $31,200 in military pensions.[7] In a few years, we will have reached the point where the interest on the national debt will be the largest part of the federal budget—larger than Medicare, larger than Social Security, larger than defense. Even under the rosiest predictions, the national debt will soon be over 100 percent of the country's entire gross domestic product. When that point comes, kiss the American dollar goodbye; the end of all that overspending will be devastating inflation, and the middle class of America will (once again) take it on the chin (see Figure P.1.).

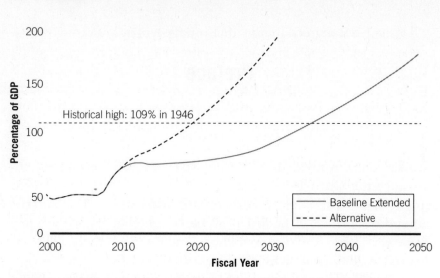

Figure P.1   Debt Held by the Public under the Two Different Social Security, Medicare, and Medicaid Projections
Source: GAO.

As Ronald Reagan remarked, "The nine most terrifying words in the English language are: 'I'm from the government and I'm here to help.'"

Just by the fact that you've invested in a book like this, I know you share my concern and I hope that you will do all you can to oppose the crazy government taxing, borrowing, and spending patterns that are leading to the ruin of the dollar and the coming dollar hyperinflation.

But enough about politics.

What This Book Is (and Isn't) About

This book is neither an economic treatise nor specific investment advice. It is intended as a resource to help empower you, the citizen, to take action and protect your money from the coming government-induced hyperinflation.

I contend hyperinflation is coming because creating and allowing inflation is the most likely strategy the politicians have for getting us out of the mess they have created. While there is broad agreement among economists that inflation pressures are growing, there is a wide variety of estimates as to what that inflation rate will be. Whether you are expecting a "mild" degree of inflation, like 5 to 10 percent, a return to 1970s-style inflation of 13 percent, or a total dollar meltdown with inflation running to hundreds or thousands of percent, there are strategies in this book for you to use.

- If you are mildly concerned about inflation, for instance, you might consider shifting some of your dollars out of bank accounts and CDs into stocks and mutual funds (described later) that may prosper during an inflationary period. You can reduce your exposure to changing interest rates by gradually cutting up your credit cards and refinancing your house to a fixed rate, rather than a variable rate, loan.
- If you are a little more wary about the future climate, you probably will also want to stock up on precious metals like gold and silver, and invest in timber, oil, or other resources that are likely to hold their value.
- If you are really worried about the direction of the economy, you can start to plan now to weather a depression-like period. Buying land in the country, moving assets overseas, and stocking up on food and medical supplies all are reasonable moves if things get really bad.

The book is organized around four major principles that will help you protect your money:

Principle 1 states "exchange dollars for real things." Here you'll learn about tangible investments that hold their value when paper currencies fail. You've probably heard about gold, oil, and real estate—but what about timber? Diamonds? Stamps? Art?

Principle 2 tells us that "future money is cheap money." In an inflationary environment, how should you handle your mortgage? Credit cards? Student debt?

Principle 3 suggests "diversify out of dollars." The dollar used to be a house built of bricks; now it's a house of straw. But is the euro any better? The yuan? And how can you protect government-regulated accounts like your IRA or 401(k)?

Finally, *principle 4* encourages us to "prepare for the worst, but expect the best." Taxes are almost certain to skyrocket in the coming decade, and in a world with a rapidly disintegrating dollar, it may be prudent to develop useful skills or stock up your country retreat.

Time to Take Action

I'm afraid that the outlook for our country is very gloomy indeed, but that doesn't mean we need to throw in the towel. In this book, I've tried to gather into one place all the different ways a person can begin to "inflation-proof" his or her life savings. No one needs to be a victim of misguided government policies; you can take action now to hold on to what you have and protect your assets from what is almost sure to be a prolonged bout of severe inflation.

Here are just a few of the things you'll discover in this book:

- Why you are late to the gold party
- Why silver is undervalued
- What coins to have on hand
- Is now the time to make your housing move?
- Is the world running out of oil?
- How to profit from the oil supply chain
- Why you should stay away from palladium
- How to get money to grow on trees
- Why fixed-rate mortgages are your friend
- What to do if your house is in foreclosure
- Why credit cards aren't worth the plastic they're printed on
- What currencies should you invest in?
- How to become a foreign farmer
- The threat to your IRA wealth
- When not to convert to a Roth IRA
- How to turn a $700,000 tax bill into $10 million tax-free gift

- The warning signs of an imminent currency collapse
- Is the United States the next Greece?
- The lesson of the Russian grandmothers
- Why whisky and pot are your depression friends
- The health care bomb: Why you'd better have that surgery now
- How to maintain your privacy in a Facebook world

Inflation-Proof Your Portfolio

The Dollar's Shrinking Value

As the U.S. government racks up a national debt approaching the size of the entire economy, something's got to give. When the public debt of approximately $15 trillion is added to the $50 trillion guaranteed for Medicare, Medicaid, Social Security, and other guarantees related to the 2008–2009 bailouts, the government is on the hook for as much as $100 trillion.[1] Increased taxes and budget cutting just won't make a dent in obligations of this size. When the bill comes due, expect massive inflation.

Why Governments Love Inflation

Inflation occurs when a government coins money faster than society creates wealth. The government, with its insiders and elites, is both the cause of and the primary beneficiary of inflation.

To see why, consider the past, when money was linked to metal coins made out of gold or silver. In ancient Rome, a denarius was at first almost 100 percent pure silver. Gradually, the Roman government reduced the amount of silver in the denarius until it contained only 5 percent silver. The hyperinflation induced by the currency manipulation made it impossible for the government to collect taxes in a timely fashion and led to this familiar scenario:

> At first, the government could raise additional revenue from the sale of state property. Later, more unscrupulous emperors

like Domitian (81–96 A.D.) would use trumped-up charges to confiscate the assets of the wealthy. They would also invent excuses to demand tribute from the provinces and the wealthy.[2]

By debasing the currency, the Roman emperors were able to pay off government debts by forcing their citizens to accept coins that had less and less precious metal content. The debased coins were worth less, forcing citizens to spend more and more denarii to buy basic goods. In other words, debasing the currency caused inflation.

"It Can't Happen Here"—or Can It?

Today a similar debasing process is going on with American money. Once a U.S. dime was 90 percent silver; now it is 0 percent silver. Until 1934, a U.S. dollar bought an ounce of gold for the fixed rate of $20.67. Now it costs over $1,500 to buy an ounce of gold.[3]

Taxes: Your Money or Your Life

"To actually finance the President's current spending plans, taxes would have to rise 20 percent across the board over the next decade and 60 percent over the next 25 years."

The U.S. dollar is almost certain to have a sustained run of extremely high inflation over the next decade because of continued huge government deficits and unfunded liabilities like the recent health care reform. To actually finance the President's current spending plans, taxes would have to rise 20 percent across the board over the next decade and 60 percent over the next 25 years.[4] Even before the health care makeover, the Petersen-Pew Commission on Budget Reform warned that in 2009 alone, the national debt shot up from 41 to 53 percent of the gross domestic product (GDP). The Commission expects the debt to reach 100 percent of the GDP by 2022 and 200 percent by 2038.[5]

In other words, in just a few years our nation will owe twice as much as it produces. We've run up the credit card to owe double what we earn in a year. Since no conceivable level of taxes and borrowing will enable the United States to service such an enormous debt, the cowardly political way to deal with the situation will be to allow inflation to run rampant.

How Low Can It Go?

What will happen is that more and more dollars will be pumped into the economy—far more money growth than the underlying economic growth rate would justify. The newly printed money will gradually be worth less and less. But legally, holders of U.S. obligations are forced to accept the devalued dollars. This is exactly the same trick the Roman emperors used.

It's a trick that works really well as long as inflation is so slow—a few percent per year—that people don't really notice. But if the supply of money grows too quickly, the inflation rate can become very high very fast. (It would be hard not to notice the 25.8 percent loss of purchasing power consumers are experiencing in Venezuela this year, for instance.[6]) And if citizens completely lose faith in the value of a currency, the inflation rate can shoot up to hundreds or even thousands of percent per month, effectively making paper currency worthless.

This happened in Germany in 1923, where paper money became so worthless that people burned it in furnaces instead of firewood, stuffed it in their clothing for insulation, and used it to paper their walls (see Figure 1.1).

"My father was a lawyer, and he had taken out an insurance policy in 1903," said German oil consultant Walter Levy. "Every month he had made the payments faithfully. It was a 20-year policy, and when it came due, he cashed it in and bought a single loaf of bread."[7]

In Zimbabwe in 2008, inflation ran so far out of control (over 79 million percent per month at one point) that at its height, the government was printing $100 trillion bills—which "couldn't buy a bus ticket in the capital of Harare," reports the *Wall Street Journal*.[8, 9]

Figure 1.1   Paper-Hanging in Weimar Germany
Source: Deutsches Bundesarchiv (German Federal Archive), Bild 102–00104.

What You Don't Notice Won't Upset You

The dollar is already shrinking, but so slowly most of us don't notice. The loss in dollar purchasing power only becomes obvious over long stretches of time.

Have you ever been in a gift shop and seen one of those little nostalgia booklets with quaint ads from, say, 25 years ago? They usually contain a section showing the wacky prices we paid for common items way back when. Table 1.1 offers a look back at 1986.

The Consumer Price Index is the government's indicator of the dollar's declining worth over time. The Bureau of Labor Statistics keeps track of the value of a basket of goods and services purchased by urban households. While the figures may not be entirely reliable, they have the value of being consistently kept since 1913. Table 1.2 shows what it costs to buy what a dollar bought in 1913.

Table 1.1 25-Year Change in Cost

Item	Cost in 1986	Cost in 2011
A five-gallon can of gasoline	$ 4.45	$17.85
A book of twenty First Class postage stamps	$ 4.40	$ 8.80
A movie ticket	$ 3.71	$ 7.97
A Hersey bar (1.65 oz.)	$ 0.40	$ 1.00
A box of Kellogg's Corn Flakes (18 oz.)	$ 1.39	$ 5.68
A package of Oreo cookies (20 oz.)	$ 1.69	$ 6.78
Pair of Major League Baseball tickets	$12.42	$42.80
Total	$28.46	$90.88

Sources: boxofficemojo.com, foodtimeline.org, eia.doe.gov, thepeoplehistory.gov.

Table 1.2 Erosion of Dollar Purchasing Power, 1913–2011

Year	Dollars Needed to Maintain $1 in Purchasing Power
1913	1.00
1920	2.02
1925	1.77
1930	1.69
1935	1.38
1940	1.41
1945	1.82
1950	2.43
1955	2.71
1960	2.99
1965	3.18
1970	3.92
1975	5.43
1980	8.32
1985	10.87
1990	13.20
1995	15.39
2000	17.39

(*continued*)

Table 1.2   Erosion of Dollar Purchasing Power, 1913–2011 (*continued*)

Year	Dollars Needed to Maintain $1 in Purchasing Power
2001	17.89
2002	18.17
2003	18.59
2004	19.08
2005	19.73
2006	20.18
2007	20.94
2008	21.57
2009	21.67
2010	22.03
2011	22.92

Source: Bureau of Labor Statistics, http://stats.bls.gov/.

Except for the Depression years (when prices came down as the economy lost steam and producers had to chase the dollars of reluctant-to-spend consumers), the dollar has steadily eroded in value. Overall, it costs roughly twice as much to live in 2011 as it did in 1986. If you haven't doubled your salary since then, your standard of living is going down.

How Much Was That Doggie in the Window?

For more fun facts about the costs of common items from year to year, visit www.thepeoplehistory.com. And if you want to play around with inflation numbers, www.usinflationcalculator.com offers a calculator based on government CPI data.

Inflation Is Already Picking Up Steam

Although it may take years for our out-of-control spending habits to bring about a U.S. currency collapse, the inflation process has begun.

Food prices are up. Holidays provide a quick reality check for inflation: The *Daily Mail* calculated that the cost of a Memorial Day cookout in 2011 was 29 percent higher than it was a year earlier, with lettuce up 28 percent, tomatoes 86 percent, and ground beef up 12.1 percent in that period.[10] And *Bloomberg Businessweek* reports that the cost of Thanksgiving in 2011 was up 13 percent, with turkey prices up 22 percent and higher prices for peas, milk, stuffing, and pumpkin pie.[11]

While falling home prices and low interest rates make housing a buyer's market for those with the money and credit, rental housing is more unaffordable for many with declining incomes.[12] The Census Bureau reports a 4 percent rise in renters in the year ending June 2011, as homeownership declines and younger renters postpone buying.[13]

Rising cotton, transportation, and labor costs are driving up the price of clothing. Gap Inc. reported its costs up 20 percent in the second half of 2011.[14] In 2011, apparel prices increased at their fastest rate since 1992—up almost 4 percent in the spring quarter.[15]

Higher prices for gasoline are also draining America's wallets. Prices jumped 37 percent in the spring of 2011 and more than 25 percent of Americans think prices may rise another 75 cents or more.[16] Experts agree. Bob van der Valk, a fuel price specialist, says, "We started high on gasoline prices this year and we stayed high, and we are going to go higher next year." Van der Valk is predicting prices as high as $4.50 a gallon in California by Easter.[17]

And the cost of health insurance rose 9 percent in 2011, with many businesses declining to hire as health costs go up.[18] Insurers are anticipating higher costs under Obamacare mandates, though of course the White House attributes the increase to "high insurance company profits."[19]

A Hope Is Not a Plan

Already $11 trillion in stimulus and bailout money has been committed to be pumped into the economy—money that is being borrowed and eventually must be paid back. The sheer profligacy of the effort—which includes everything from bailing out AIG to paying car buyers for their junk cars—boggles the mind.

Where Your Money Went: The 2008 Bailout

Program	Description	Committed	Invested
Troubled Asset Relief Program	Financial rescue to restore liquidity to the financial markets	$ 700 billion	$356.2 billion
Federal Reserve Rescue Efforts	Financial rescue to restore liquidity to the financial markets	$ 6.4 trillion	$ 1.5 trillion
Federal Stimulus Programs	Programs designed to save or create jobs and prevent recession	$ 1.2 trillion	$577.8 billion
American International Group	Bailout to help insurer restructure and get rid of toxic assets	$ 182 billion	$127.4 billion
FDIC Bank Takeovers	Cost to FDIC fund that insures banks	$45.4 billion	
Other Financial Initiatives	Additional programs designed to rescue the financial sector	$ 1.7 trillion	$366.4 billion
Housing Initiatives	Programs designed to rescue the housing market and prevent foreclosures	$ 745 billion	$130.6 billion
Grand Total		**$ 11 trillion**	**$ 3 trillion**

Source: David Goldman, "CNNMoney.com's Bailout Tracker," CNNMoney, November 16, 2009, http://money.cnn.com/news/storysupplement/economy/bailouttracker/index.html (accessed February 22, 2012).

On top of the bailout, add in more trillions for health care programs, Social Security, and other entitlements, and an economic disaster is in the making.

The government has three main strategies to pay off all these obligations: stimulate the economy to phenomenal heights, raise taxes to unsustainable levels, or get foreigners to finance larger and larger deficits through sales of Treasury bonds.

None of this is going to happen.

The stimulus money is not stimulating the economy because it's really just government spending, not aimed at anything productive (like helping businesses buy new equipment so they can be more competitive). If taxes are raised to ridiculous levels, businesses will flee the country or stop bothering to produce, because the government will be taking all the profits. And foreigners, like the Chinese and the Saudis, can see where the United States is heading and so are already pulling back on buying U.S. government bonds.

There is, however, a fourth way out of the debt mess—devalue the dollar through inflation. It's the way the Roman emperors chose to solve their spending problems and the way the U.S. government seems intent to follow—in fact, even if not by intent (see Figure 1.2).

St. Louis Federal Reserve President James Bullard said, for instance, that one of effects of the "QE2" stimulus was to weaken the dollar. St. Louis Fed economist Christopher Neely estimated that the dollar depreciated 6.5 percent overall and 11 percent

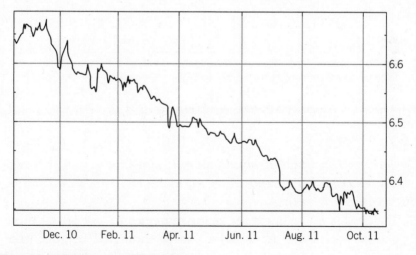

Figure 1.2   U.S. Dollar versus Chinese Yuan

Source: www.advfn.com.

against the Japanese yen.[20] And China and the United States apparently made a secret deal in January 2011 to allow the dollar to weaken against the yuan, resulting in a steadily falling dollar.

A hope is not a plan. So while our politicians have adopted a policy of hoping everything will turn out okay, it would be prudent for the average citizen to plan what to do in case it does not.

1

Exchange Dollars for Real Things

In a world where dollars are dropping in value over time, it's not smart to hoard dollars.

My Uncle John, an Italian immigrant who arrived in the United States during the Great Depression, spent the rest of his life hoarding cash, literally hiding it away in boxes kept under the bed. Did his strategy do him any good? No. A $100 bill he saved in 1933 was only worth $9 in buying power when he died in 1988.

He would have done much better buying a house. The average price of a house in 1933 was $5,750. That same house in the year of his death (1988) cost $91,000[1]—an appreciation rate of 5.15 percent. By contrast, $5,750 stuck under Uncle John's mattress for 55 years would have bought only $517 worth of flowers for his funeral.

Inflation had destroyed over 90 percent of his savings' value.

Because inflation, the subtle thief, gradually erodes money's value, in a time of big inflation it's smart to be "out" of dollars. Principle #1 says convert your dollars into things of tangible value.

Fake Dollars Demand Real Assets

"Things are tangible if you can touch, taste, smell, and feel them. They are, in other words, real."

Things are tangible if you can touch, taste, smell, and feel them. They are, in other words, real. Land, machinery, gold, and plant equipment are examples of real things.

Being real and useful, tangible assets have an intrinsic value that makes them valuable in and of themselves. For instance, let's say you own a John Deere tractor. It has a certain value to anyone who wants to plow a field, whether now or in the future. If inflation wipes out the value of the dollar, the value of that tractor as a field-plowing machine still remains. In an inflationary future, it will cost more dollars to buy or lease a tractor, and if the dollar were to collapse altogether, farmers would still trade something of value for the use of a tractor at planting time. The tractor's value is intrinsic.

For the purpose of protecting your wealth against inflation, consider owning a basket of investments in tangible things: gold, silver, oil, real estate, and other commodities.

CHAPTER

Life in the Gold Rush?

In a world awash with monetary stimulus, investors have increasingly turned to gold as a hedge against economic and political mayhem. Under worldwide buying pressure from financiers and central banks, prices have risen, but have further to go as the dollar weakness becomes apparent.

Silver is the other major precious metal with investing characteristics similar to gold. Both gold and silver can be purchased as coins, bullion, or through exchange-traded funds. You may even want to take physical possession of your precious metals to guard against fraud, bankruptcy, or coercive government actions.

Gold: Traditional Haven for Nervous Investors

Traditionally, gold has been the haven that nervous investors turn to when frightened about the strength of the dollar. Gold coinage has been money for at least 5,000 years. Gold is the one inflation hedge most people have heard of—especially now that it's relentlessly promoted on radio and television.

All you have to do is look at the massive rise in gold prices since the turn of the century—from around $275 to about $1,550 per ounce—to see how fear of the inflationary economy has affected the price of gold (see Figure 2.1).

Gold bugs will point to numerous reasons you should own gold, and why its price will go to $2,000 or even $10,000 an ounce. Its use

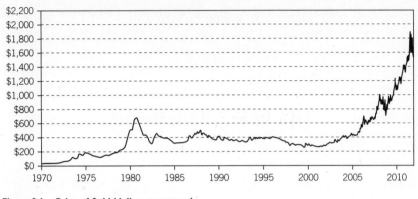

Figure 2.1　Price of Gold (dollars per ounce)
Source: World Gold Council.

in industry for electronics, computers, and aerospace is increasing.[2] Demand from countries like India and China are driving prices up. (India alone consumed 657 tons of gold in 2010.[3]) Central banks and the International Monetary Fund have begun buying again after years of indifference.[4] Gold has gained value for 11 straight years, up 26 percent in the first 11 months of 2011.[5, 6]

Caution: You Are Late to the Gold Party

However, before you plunge into the gold market, be aware of some golden pitfalls.

First of all, you are coming late to the party. You can already see the upward gold price trend sputtering a bit in Figure 2.1. Hundreds of thousands of nervous investors have been pouring their dollars into gold. High demand = high price. The Reserve Bank of India came into the market in the second quarter of 2009 and bought 200 metric tons of gold from the International Monetary Fund.[7] And China's investment demand surged 70 percent in 2010, according to Albert Cheng of the World Gold Council.

Other figures from the Council show that 57 percent of the world's gold over the past five years was used for jewelry and another 11 percent for industry. That leaves 31 percent to be used for investment purposes. And because the supply of gold has remained relatively stable in recent years, changes in gold price are most closely related to investor demand.

In other words, one of the main reasons the price of gold rises or falls is that investors expect it to. Gold prices rise out of fear, greed, and market sentiment as much as they do out of underlying factors like inflation.

Beware Investors Fleeing Gold

Because gold is seen as a financial refuge, it can rise rapidly when financial markets are nervous, but also fall rapidly when financial fears ease. Sometimes the refuge aspect of gold ownership isn't much help if weakness in other markets forces investors' hands.

This behavior was apparent following the August 2011 stock market fall. Gold had reached a record high of $1,888 an ounce that month as investors tried to avoid cash dollars in the wake of the S&P downgrade of U.S. credit—then plunged 11 percent in value over the next few weeks.[8]

Why? As stock prices fell, investors facing losses sold gold to raise funds, putting downward pressure on the price. Investors who expected gold to go up when the stock market went down got burned. (Long-term institutional investors, however, stayed in the game and gold has begun trending upward again, though not at its previous highs.) Because many investors buy gold to balance off risks they perceive in the stock market, gold may prove volatile at precisely the moment markets tank.

Why to Buy Some Gold Anyway

Gold is widely recognized as an alternative to paper currency. Until 1934, don't forget, the dollar was backed by gold at $20.67 per ounce, which shows how deflated the dollar has become relative to this coveted commodity.

So should you buy gold? Yes, because as the world becomes awash with cheapened dollars, the value of the dollar is bound to fall. Gold is the historical fallback position for a weakened dollar. In fact, since gold prices have been allowed to float against the dollar in the 1970s, the two have moved in inverse step, with gold going up when the dollar goes down, and vice versa.[9]

Central banks (like that of India cited previously) have been expanding their gold reserves. Banks of smaller countries like Thailand, Bolivia, and Tajikistan have also gotten into the act, buying up a combined 18.2 metric tons in 2011.[10] Further, central banks have apparently bought up an additional 150 tons, but secretly, to avoid pushing up the market. Says Marcus Grubb, managing director of the World Gold Council:

> While one can account for some of the purchases—from Thailand, Bolivia, Russia etcetera—there is an unaccounted amount out there. A clue probably lies in the fact that a lot of [recent] buying has been from central banks that have been in surplus, [in regions] like Asia and Latin America.[11]

Gold's biggest single use is the manufacturing of jewelry, which is often purchased as much for its intrinsic gold value as its beauty. As prices have risen, demand for gold jewelry fell by 10 percent overall in volume (even while rising 24 percent in price), though demand is still strong in China, where it rose 13 percent. And though the weak global economy has stifled demand for electronics, gold is an irreplaceable metal in its manufacturing processes and its use remained constant in 2011.[12]

If you do decide to make gold part of your inflation-hedging strategy, don't put all of your money into gold (for that matter, don't put all of your money into any of the strategies recommended in this book). Instead, review the many hyperinflation investment options described in this book and decide how you will apportion available investment dollars.

According to a study conducted by New Frontier Advisors and the World Gold Council, a 1 to 2 percent allocation of gold in a low-risk portfolio or 2 to 4 percent in a balanced-risk portfolio is an appropriate level of diversification (comparable to small-cap or emerging markets funds).[13]

On the other hand, research conducted by Brad Zigler, managing editor of Hard Assets Investor, concludes, "Giving over 20 percent of one's portfolio to gold, for example, would have cranked up average returns . . . for all but the longest interval—while significantly dampening volatility."[14]

Buying Gold Now

However much gold you decide to buy, you will need a strategy for entering the market. You will want to avoid, of course, jumping in with a lump-sum purchase at what might prove in hindsight to be a market high.

One way to buy gold in a hot market is to "buy on the dips." Like stocks and other commodities, gold prices tend to fluctuate in three-, five-, and eight-day patterns that provide opportunities to buy gold at a discounted sale price.

Another approach to buying gold in a volatile market is to work your way into a position using dollar cost averaging. This involves making equal weekly, monthly, or quarterly purchases in a specific time frame (studies indicate 6 to 12 months of time is best). Market risk is thus minimized because although sometimes you are purchasing gold at highs (with a chance to fall), at other times you are purchasing gold at lows (with a chance to appreciate). You are forgoing some possibility of appreciation for the insurance of getting your gold at an average selling price.

Gold Supply and Demand

Because the dollar is no longer traded at a government-fixed price in gold, the price of gold it is set by the balance of supply and demand. Gold demand is based on its uses in industry, jewelry, and dentistry, as well as for investment. Gold supply consists of gold already refined as well as new supplies entering the market from the mines (see Table 2.1).

Since 2003, the largest source of growth in demand has been in the investment sector as investors seek stability for their wealth. Mine production of gold has remained relatively stable during this period[15] (see Table 2.2).

How High Will Gold Go?

Gold is destined to go higher—but how high, of course, no one really knows. Events and markets are inherently unpredictable. Gold reached an all-time high of $1,913 an ounce in August 2011, as investors worried—rightly—about the U.S. spending spree and weakness

Table 2.1   Gold Supply and Demand

Supply Flow (five-year average Q4'05 to Q3'10)

Type	Metric Tons	Percent
Mine production	2,209 t	59 percent
Recycled gold	1,323 t	35 percent
Net official sector sales	234 t	6 percent

Demand Flow (five-year average Q4'05 to Q3'10)

Jewelry	2,151 t	57 percent
Investment	1,182 t	31 percent
Industrial	433 t	11 percent

Source: World Gold Council.

Table 2.2   Above-Ground Gold Stocks (as of 12/31/09)

Type	Metric Tons	Percent
Jewelry	83,700 t	51 percent
Investment	29,600 t	18 percent
Official sector	28,900 t	17 percent
Industrial	19,800 t	12 percent
Unaccounted for	3,600 t	2 percent

Source: World Gold Council.

in the global economy. Prices have since settled back to the $1,750 mark—a phenomenal rise from $280 a decade ago.[16]

How high will gold go? Here are some predictions made over the last year, compiled from a variety of financial sources. As you can see, a few of the benchmarks have already been hit.

- Investment advisor Gil Morales predicts a price of $2,000 by the end of 2011. "All they're going to do in Europe is kick the can down the road, and that means more printing of more fiat money," he said.[17]
- Barclays Capital was also forecasting prices around $2,000 per ounce for 2012: "We expect prices to average $1,875 per

ounce in the fourth quarter 2011 and $2,000 per ounce on an annual average basis in 2012 as the macro insecurity [in Europe] persists," says Suki Cooper, a Barclays analyst.[18]

- Rich Bourquard, CEO of Investment Arts Corporation, sees two counterbalanced forces operating on gold's price: economic uncertainty such as euro or yen instability on one hand, and the rush to dollars as the "last major currency standing— over the coming year I see these two opposing forces roughly counterbalancing each other, producing a gold value of around $2,000 USD/troy ounce."[19]

- A September 2011 poll of traders, analysts, miners, and central bankers from the London Bullion Market Association predicts that the price of gold bullion will rise about 12 percent in 2012 to $2,019 an ounce. Said delegate Peter Marrone, CEO of Yamana Gold, "I'm a big believer that all of the ingredients for a higher gold price are there: geopolitical risk, economic uncertainty, inflation."[20]

- Morgan Stanley analysts increased their 2012 forecast for gold 35 percent, to $2,464 per ounce. "Gold, and silver to a much lesser extent, are viewed as safe havens and store of value as well as the closest thing to a global reserve currency," the report said.[21]

- Citigroup analyst Heath Jansen foresees a hunger if euro and dollar problems continue: "On a worst-case scenario for euro sovereign debt and USA fiscal problems, we believe gold could repeat the extent of the 1970–1980 gold bull market, implying upside risk to above $2,500 an ounce."[22]

- "I'd be real disappointed if gold wasn't in excess of $2,500 in the next 12 months," said John Embry of Sprott Asset Management. Embry successfully predicted current trading ranges a year in advance.[23]

- Boston money manager Antony Herrey estimates that gold could hit $5,000 an ounce if it reaches its highs of 1980 adjusted for inflation.[24]

Which of these forecasts is the most accurate? At the height of a financial crisis, all of these price points may be exceeded, and more, as people realize their dollars are rapidly becoming worthless. Mark Lundeen and James Turk have compared the amount of gold the United States holds to the number of U.S. dollars in circulation. The ratio? Almost $54,000 per ounce as of the end of 2010.[25]

There are, I should note, pessimists who are predicting gold's luster will soon fade:

- Bank of America strategist MacNeil Curry forecasts prices in the range of $1,462–$1,576 per ounce based on similarities to 2006 technical trading signals.[26]
- Christoph Eible, CEO of the Swiss hedge fund Tiberius Group, warns that gold could fall back below $1,000 an ounce—close to its production costs.[27]
- Nouriel Roubini, a professor of economics at New York University, sees gold as falling 50 percent or more. "The higher they go the harder they'll crash," he says, calling current gold prices a "bubble."[28]

Make a pick and put your money down. Personally, I'm betting with the bulls.

The Easy Way to Buy Gold

The easiest, fastest, and cheapest way to buy gold is through an exchange-traded fund (ETF). An ETF is like a mutual fund for owning gold and can be purchased through any stock brokerage account like Ameritrade or E-Trade.

The most successful gold ETF is the SPDR Gold Shares Fund, which goes by the stock symbol GLD. Started in 2004, GLD already holds for investors over 36 million ounces of gold—more than the central banks of Brazil or South Korea.[29] Its price is modeled on the price of 1/10 ounce of gold, and was selling at $164.77 in late November 2011. Expenses are low—0.4 percent per year—and the gold is physically held by the fund at various locations. You can read the prospectus at http://www.spdrgoldshares.com/media/GLD/file/SPDRGoldTrustProspectus.pdf.

Another gold ETF is the iShares COMEX Gold Trust. The iShares symbol is IAU. It holds more than 5.5 million ounces of gold in trust for its customers, and has the same low expense ratio as its competitor GLD.

Buying and selling gold using an ETF is as easy as buying and selling a stock. There is no need to take physical possession and thus no expenses connected to transporting and storing your gold.

Downsides of Exchange-Traded Funds

Although ETFs are convenient, they do have downsides you should take into account. While you should have no problem buying or selling popular ETFs like GLD or IAU, some obscure ETFs are thinly traded, leading to spreads (difference between the asking and selling prices) of up to $2.50 per share, compared to the usual nickel or less. Such large spreads are the result of an illiquid market, meaning it may be difficult to sell your ETF when you want to.[30]

Occasionally, too, ETFs suspend issuing new shares because of problems associated with a flood of investor demand, which can cause share prices to drift too far from underlying asset values.

Such problems might especially arise in the case of a monetary crisis—as does the threat of government regulatory actions. Just as with money held in a bank or stocks held at a stock brokerage, in a crisis the government has the ability to ration your access to, or even shut down, your account.

Finally, ETF records are subject to subpoena and inspection, and thus your privacy can be compromised. The Right to Financial Privacy Act requires government agencies to provide notice and an opportunity to object before a financial institution can disclose your financial information to a government agency, but the burden is on you to opt out of provisions that may be hidden in paperwork provided by your institution.[31, 32] Some courts have concluded that you have no reasonable expectation of privacy with respect to information you provide to third parties over the Internet.[33]

Warning: Exchange-Traded Notes = Added Risks

Cousin investments to exchange-traded funds are exchange-traded notes, or ETNs. While buyers of ETFs are buying into a basket of securities, purchasers of ETNs are buying into a basket of notes—that is, unsecured debt instruments. This exposes the buyer to the additional risks of failed payments and of bankruptcies—certainly a possibility when credit markets are roiled.

For instance, when Lehman Brothers failed, trading was halted in its three ETNs (the Opta Lehman Commodity ETN, the Agricultural ETN, and the Private Equity ETN). Holders of Lehman ETNs lost 98 cents of every dollar of their investment. Bear Stearns ETN holders barely missed meeting the same fate.[34]

Because ETNs are likely to run into trouble precisely when the economy weakens, they are a bad bet as a dollar hedge.

Why You Should Have Some Physical Gold

In the event of a "bank holiday," your assets could be held hostage while politicians decide how to regain order. It happened under FDR in 1933 and happened again most recently in Argentina, where bank customers were restricted as to when and how much money they could access from their accounts.

Another scenario that might cause gold in your account to disappear is the failure of the private firm holding it. In the winter of 2011, as broker-dealer MF Global wavered on the brink of bankruptcy, the company looted its customers' holdings of 1.2 billion dollars, illegally transferring them to its own account.[35] Then, as Chapter 11 trustees took control of the firm, even fully-funded customers were hit with repeated margin calls when their assets were frozen. Trends forecaster Gerald Calente—who reportedly lost a six-figure gold account in the scandal—called the moves "economic martial law."[36]

The Strong Arm of the Law

"In the event of a 'bank holiday,' your assets could be held hostage while politicians decide how to regain order."

The only insurance against such legal and illegal disasters is to actually have control of your gold as a physical asset, in the form of coins or bullion. Taking physical possession of your gold may be inconvenient (where can you store it to ensure access when you need it?) and expose you to other risks (theft, natural disasters)—but puts you firmly in control when push comes to shove.

Another advantage to physical possession of your precious metal investments: You have control over your property and know exactly what you are holding. There is no room for counterparty shenanigans, such as, say, a fraudster selling the same physical gold to multiple parties.

To avoid ending up the victim of private or public financial malfeasance, it's simply prudent to hold at least a portion of your wealth as gold physically in your possession.

What Coins to Have on Hand

Coins are tangible, portable, come in various sizes, and will hold their own as a store of value through good times and bad. Hard to believe, but gold coins were the norm here in America, redeemable for decades at $20.67 through 1934, when FDR went to work under-cutting gold's value to finance his social policies.[37]

Stick with widely recognized coinage of known weights. The U.S. Gold Eagle, the South African Krugerrand, and the Canadian Maple Leaf are the safest bets. Each of these coins contains a troy ounce of gold and is widely traded around the world. Other coins to consider are the Australian Kangaroo, the Chinese Panda, and the U.S. Buffalo.

When buying gold coins, be aware that you will incur expenses that include a dealer markup over the spot price and costs of insuring, shipping, and storing your coins. Comparison shop dealers by asking for their "out-the-door price," which will roll commissions, shipping, and insurance costs together.

Why to Avoid Bullion

Gold is also available in bullion (bar) form in weights ranging from 1, 10, 100, and 400 troy ounces as well as one kilo (32.15 troy ounces). One problem with such bars is that they are large and not easily divided should the occasion arise, but more importantly, they are not as widely traded and may have to be assayed during an exchange—an additional cost and delay. By contrast, the gold coins recommended above tend to be smaller in denomination and widely recognized and accepted.

If you do trade bullion, look for bars bearing serial numbers of Johnson Matthey and Credit Suisse.

How to Buy Mining Stocks (If You Must)

Another, indirect, way to own gold is to own publicly traded stocks in gold mining companies. Mining companies have hundreds of thousands or millions of ounces of gold in the ground, and as gold prices rise, so does the intrinsic price of gold mining companies.

By buying mining stocks (or a mutual fund that invests in a portfolio of such companies), you are taking a bigger risk than buying gold outright, because corporate and geopolitical problems can derail the mining process. So gold mining stocks are leveraged investments that tend to go up—and down—faster than the price of gold.

Because you can own gold outright and get the inflation protection benefits, investing in mining stocks is more speculative than protective. Like any company, a mining company can be the subject of poor management or even of government takeover, as recently happened in Venezuela when Hugo Chavez decreed the nationalization of Venezuela's gold mining sector.[38]

If, despite the risks, you do decide to buy mining stocks, look for a mutual fund with diversified holdings to limit your exposure to any one stock. A few mining mutual funds to consider: the Midas Fund (symbol: MIDSK), the USAA Precious Metals and Mineral Funds (symbol: USAGX), Franklin Gold and Precious Metals (symbol: FKRCX) and the Van Eck's Market Vectors Gold Miners EFT (symbol: GDX).

Silver—the Other White Meat

Silver is gold's monetary twin. Like gold, it has a long history of use in jewelry and coinage. In ancient Lydia, silver was alloyed with gold to form coins as long ago as 700 B.C. The British pound gets its name from the fact that it once represented the value of one pound of silver. Silver was used in U.S. coinage until 1964, when inflation made silver coins worth more than their face value.

Why Silver Is Undervalued

Silver, like gold, is subject to price volatility, but has gradually been moving up in price since around 2004, when it traded for $6.67 per troy ounce. By March 2008, silver was trading for almost $20 per troy ounce before falling back to a range of about $17 to $19 per troy ounce. In 2010, silver took another big leap to an all-time high of $49.51, and in November 2011 it was trading in the low 30s.

Silver, however, is still undervalued compared to gold. Silver has many industrial uses for which there is no simple substitute, such as applications in batteries, circuits, and electronic components. Such demand accounts for over 50 percent of the application of silver, and therefore sets a base value. It also accounts for the reason that silver prices tend to dip in a recession, where industrial output slackens.

It also, however, portends an uptick in silver prices when the economy begins to rebound. Because silver also has a monetary component, it tends to move up and down in price in tandem with gold, and to maintain a certain ratio of relative value. Over the last century, this ratio has varied from about 32:1 in 1900 to about 60:1 in 2008. In 2011, the ratio was around 40:1.[39]

Currently, silver is undervalued relative to gold because of slumping industrial demand and recent steep price increases in gold. According to figures supplied by the Silver Institute and the CPM Group, there is seven times as much refined gold above ground as refined silver.[40]

"While this sounds like an outrageous claim, silver is actually rarer than gold," says investment advisor George Maniere. "This is because silver has industrial applications and every day our technologies require more and more silver to operate. Silver that is above the ground has been diminished by 91 percent since 1980, while the stockpile of gold has grown 600 percent."[41]

Industrial demand for silver rose almost 21 percent in 2010, while mine production rose by only 2.5 percent, meaning more silver is consumed each year in industrial processes than is being mined. Add to this pressure from investors—world silver investment was up 40 percent in 2010—and the price of silver seems destined to continue a long-term rise.[42]

The Pros and Cons of Holding Silver Coins and Bullion

As with gold, silver can be physically held in the form of bullion or coins. Because silver costs less than gold, at the current ratio of 40:1, you will need 40 times as much storage space to hold an equivalent store of value in your safe or safety deposit box. Add costs to transport or ship silver coins and storage costs become significant compared to gold.

Silver bullion should be avoided for the same reason as gold bullion: The large bars are not easily traded and may need to be assayed before sale. If you do decide to buy bullion, stick to reputable brands like Engelhard and Johnson Matthey.

Fine silver coins are sold by the same dealers that handle gold coins. The Canadian Silver Maple Leaf is an example of a widely circulated fine silver coin that is 99.99 percent pure silver. Another .999 fine silver coin is the U.S. Silver Eagle, minted in the United States since 1985.

Learning to Like "Junk"

Alternatives to fine silver coins are coins known as "junk silver," also available at coin dealers. Junk silver is older coins that used to circulate in the United States, the United Kingdom, Canada, and Australia. These coins are metal alloys containing various amounts of silver. For instance, pre-1964 U.S. half dollars, dimes, and quarters are 90 percent silver and contain 25 grams of silver per dollar of face value. Canadian silver coins from 1920 to 1967 contain 80 percent silver content.

Junk silver is sold in $1,000 face value bags, but the face value is actually irrelevant. The bags are priced on the actual silver content of the coins, with a $1,000 face value bag typically containing over 700 ounces of pure silver, depending on the actual coins involved.

Two reasons people invest in junk silver coins: First, American junk silver coins are still legal tender and thus a junk silver dime will never be worth less than 10 cents, putting a bottom-level value on the investment.

More importantly to some, in the event of extreme economic times, 90 percent silver coins are widely recognized and their small size makes them ideal for everyday bartering.

Silver coins also provide an instructive example of how inflation destroys value. The monetary value of the silver in a 1963 Franklin half dollar is currently $6.75; the monetary value of the metal in a 2010 half dollar, containing no silver? Just over five cents. See http://www.coinflation.com for more comparisons.

Another Way to Profit from Silver

Like gold, silver is now available through your stock brokerage account as exchange-traded funds. iShares Silver Trust trades on the New York Stock Exchange as SLV and was valued at almost $10 billion in late 2011.[43] Another ETF, the ETF Securities Silver Trust, trades as SIVR with a slightly lower expense ratio.

Digging for Silver

A complete list of silver ETFs is available at http://etf.stock-encyclopedia.com/category/silver-etfs.html.

Key Points

- Gold is *the* traditional hedge against currency uncertainties.
- Investor pressure has been pushing up the price of gold, but there is still life in the gold rush for a portion of your assets.
- Gold ETFs are an easy way to buy gold.
- Silver is undervalued in relation to gold.
- Avoid mining stocks and ETNs.
- Take physical possession of your metals if you are worried about fraud or government manipulation.

Real Estate: Home Is Where the Hedge Is

Real estate may be the ultimate tangible asset. While plenty of Americans lost money in the housing bubble, the bubble has burst and prices have floated back to earth. Foreclosure opportunities and cheap mortgage money now make holding property a realistic inflation hedge. In many areas of the country, housing costs have fallen below building costs and it's cheaper to buy than rent. Apartment building and farmland investments can provide cash flow and further opportunities for diversification.

Why You Should Own Your Home

Most people should own the home they live in. After all, everyone needs to live somewhere, and the money one spends on rent can go to pay the mortgage. The government gives hefty tax breaks to homeowners and the housing market is currently depressed, meaning you can get a good buy on a home.

Yes, some people who bought at the height of the bubble lost money. But as you can see from Figure 3.1, the housing price spike that started around 2000 has played itself out.

The main thing that Figure 3.1 demonstrates, however, is not that people who bought during the boom lost money, but that dollars deflate while housing holds its value.

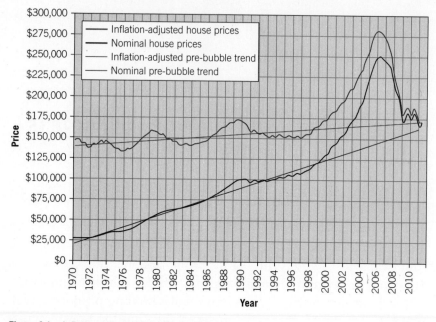

Figure 3.1   Inflation-Adjusted U.S. Housing Prices
Source: jparsons.net.

The topmost line shows that the value of houses, when adjusted for inflation (and excluding the housing bubble of the 2000s), has held roughly in the $150,000 to $175,000 range since the 1970s. The amount of dollars needed to buy a house, however (i.e., the thick bottom line), steadily rose over the decades as inflation chipped away at the dollar's value. In 2010, housing prices have reached equilibrium with the trend lines, signaling a return of pricing to historic values.

Housing is a tangible investment with a huge intrinsic utility. Whatever happens to the dollar, people still need to live somewhere. What's more, if you finance your house with a fixed-rate loan, you will be paying the mortgage in dollars of steadily declining value. And loan prices are also near historic lows.

So yes, drive a hard bargain when buying property during the current government-induced recession. But don't be so timid as to stay out of the market altogether. A home is a great place to convert your declining-value dollars into something real that you can enjoy.

With a fixed-rate mortgage and a devalued or devaluing dollar, it will actually become cheaper in relative terms as time goes on.

Is Now the Time to Make Your Housing Move?

Despite housing prices that have plunged by a third since 2006, the Fed's commitment to cheap money has driven mortgage interest rates to historic lows, turning the math in buyers' favor for the first time in a half decade. According to Moody's Analytics, prices for rentals began to increase in 2010 as demand for rental housing increased (those foreclosed homeowners have to move somewhere).[1] This means that rental prices are already beginning to inflate in some sections of the country, making the cost of owning at today's interest rates comparatively cheap.

In cities like Detroit, Miami, Dallas, Atlanta, and Phoenix, cheap mortgage money means the cost of owning can be substantially below the cost of renting. For instance, the median list price of a home in Fort Worth, Texas was $184,800 in August 2011. That's down almost 10 percent over a year earlier.

But with a 30-year fixed interest rate mortgage currently at 3.75 percent, a buyer with 20 percent down would end up paying about $684 per month. Even with property taxes, repairs, and other costs, this is less than the median rental price of $1,001—and for a larger, private home.[2]

Other cities where it currently makes sense to own are Atlanta, Detroit, Las Vegas, Miami, Minneapolis, Orlando, Phoenix, and St. Louis.[3] Local price and rental information is available at the real estate site Zillow.com, http://www.zillow.com/local-info/.

When Renting Makes More Sense

In some markets, of course, it does make more sense to rent than to own the house you live in (see Table 3.1).

Renting makes more sense so long as local home prices are still decreasing (making it wise to wait for a better deal), or because there is a huge supply of rental housing on your local market (making rents relatively cheap; see Figure 3.2.).

Table 3.1   Buy versus Rent Comparison Chart

	Advantages	Considerations
Buy	Property builds equity Sense of community, stability, and security Free to change decor and landscaping Not dependent on landlord to maintain property	Responsible for maintenance Responsible for property taxes Possibility of foreclosure and loss of equity Less mobility than renting
Rent	Little or no responsibility for maintenance Easier to move	No tax benefits No equity is built up No control over rent increases Possibility of eviction

Source: Ginniemae.gov.

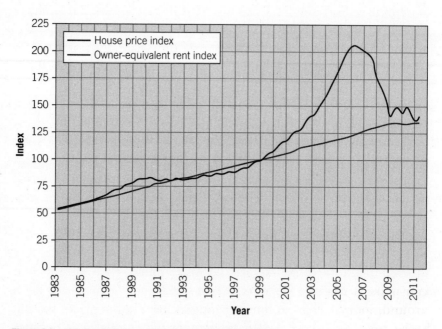

Figure 3.2   U.S. House Prices versus Owner-Equivalent Rent

Source: jparsons.net.

Renting makes the most sense when rental costs are less than ownership costs and you are disciplined enough to invest that extra money each month in inflation-proofing your future. Congress even lets you tap into your IRA tax free to help with a down payment. You (and your spouse) can each make a one-time withdrawal of $10,000 toward the purchase of a first home.[4]

Buy or Rent?

The Government National Mortgage Association (Ginnie Mae) has a nice calculator to help you decide whether renting is cheaper than buying, given local market conditions. Plug in your local numbers to see whether it makes sense to rent.
    http://www.ginniemae.gov/rent_vs_buy/rent_vs_buy_calc.asp?section= YPTH

In the long run, though, owners almost always come out ahead as they pay down their fixed-rate mortgage in dollars of steadily declining value. Keep a close eye on the market and become a buyer the moment it makes the most sense.

How to Invest in Apartment Buildings

Another strategy to divest yourself of dollars is to buy multifamily residential buildings. These can be anything from duplexes where you occupy one side and rent the other through triplexes, four-plexes, and multiunit buildings containing dozens of units.

Owning an apartment building is like owning a business. You will have to deal with renters and repairs, taxes, and building codes. However, if you buy at the right price in an area where housing is in demand, a building can provide a steady stream of income. As inflation rises, so, too, do your rents, putting you in charge of your fate.

You must be able to accurately estimate rents before you can make a realistic decision about purchasing a property. Drive around, look at comparable buildings, check newspaper ads, and make some calls pretending to be a renter. Invest in areas with strong population and economic growth where apartments are in demand and not overbuilt.

Next, determine the net operating income (NOI) for properties that interest you. Your NOI is the income you have left over after all expenses (including a vacancy allowance but excluding mortgage service and taxes) have been met. For instance, if your building earns $100,000 per year in rents (including vacancies) and has $30,000 per year in maintenance, utilities, and so on, your NOI is $70,000.

Apartment house investments need good cash flow to survive vacancies, maintenance, and repairs. The cap rate is net (not gross) income divided by the purchase price. If you buy a building for $500,000 and have $50,000 annual net operating income before taxes, the return on investment (cap rate) is 10 percent. That's way better than the current 1.6 percent rate on a CD. (On the other hand, with a CD you don't have the hassle of running a multiunit building, so build a comfort factor into your cap rate considerations to compensate for the time you'll put into your apartment business.)

Bomb Damage or Rent Control?

Before undertaking an investment in an apartment building or other rental property, make sure your building is not subject to municipal rent control. You, not the local government, need to be able to set the rents. Rent control, because it mandates rents below market value, causes housing shortages and deterioration of housing stock so severe it's indistinguishable from bomb damage.

Don't believe me? See if *you* can tell the difference. Take the "Bomb Damage or Rent Control?" challenge by Pace University economist Joseph Salerno, available on YouTube: http://www.youtube.com/watch?v=x9PUJZYzw3k.

How to Steer Clear of Passive Income Losses

The ever-hungry IRS views income from investment property as passive income and treats it in special ways in the tax code. That means that if your investment property runs a loss, you may not be able to write off the loss.

First of all, passive participants (say, a limited partner in a real estate venture) can't write off losses in the year they occur at all.

The next class of owner the IRS targets is the active partici-
pant. That's an investor who directly participates in managing
a property, but for whom real estate isn't a full-time job. If their
adjusted gross income is less than $150,000 a year, they can deduct
a portion—up to $25,000 a year—of losses. As inflation causes
more and more owners to exceed the $150,000 limit, this loophole
is slowly closing.[5]

Both active and passive participants may, however, accumu-
late unclaimed passive losses and write them off when they sell the
property.[6] As inflation causes prices to rise, though, the value of
that write-off will progressively decrease. (A $10,000 loss incurred
this year is 10 percent of the value of the property when in five
years the property becomes worth $100,000, but only 1 percent
of the value of the property when in 10 years its value rises to
$1,000,000.) You can see why the IRS loves inflation.

One sure way to avoid the IRS trap is to become what the IRS
defines as a "real estate professional," that is, someone who spends
a lot of time to "develop, redevelop, construct, reconstruct, acquire,
convert, rent, operate, manage, lease, or sell" real estate.[7] (Consult
with your tax attorney to see if you qualify.) Real estate professionals can fully deduct losses in the year they occur, protecting the
value of losses as a tax deduction from being devalued.

How to Protect Your Real Estate Equity against Falling Prices

Nervous about real estate prices? Afraid that an investment property
you buy today might be sink in value tomorrow? What if there were a
way to buy that property that locked in your equity if prices declined,
but allowed you to take advantage of all the gains if prices rose?

There is such a way. It's called a "lock in value property equity"
contract, or, more simply, a home equity protection plan. Yale economists helped develop the first such program in 2002 in Syracuse,
New York.[8] Though not insurance, it does protect against a decline
in the equity of your home by offering a compensatory payout
based on federal housing data. The cost is generally a one-time payment (at the time of the home purchase) of 1 to 3 percent of the
home cost. That's $2,000 to $6,000 on a $200,000 condo purchase,

for example. There is a lockout period of up to three years that bars you from collecting payments on a flip.[9]

Home equity protection plans are a new concept and not widely known. Two companies that offer such contracts are Equity Lock Solutions and The Lighthouse Group. If you're buying in Minnesota, check to see whether the state's proposed Homes Value Guarantee Program has passed. It will insure a buyer's down payment for five years after purchase.[10]

Invest in U.S. Farmland

You can become a farmer without getting your hands dirty by remotely investing in U.S. farmlands. According to the National Council of Real Estate Investment Fiduciaries (NCREIF), in the last 20 years farmland in the United States has never had a down year.[11]

Farmland use breaks down into two major categories: one for permanent crops like citrus, fruit, and nut trees and another for row crops like corn and soybeans. Farmland may be leased or owned, with leased farms placing more risk on the local operators.[12] USB Global Asset Management Farmland invests in U.S. farmland diversified across the country. Its annualized returns have been over 10 percent since 1991, but require a $50 million minimum investment. Ceres Partners also invests in U.S. farmland and seeks to identify and buy undervalued farm properties. Ceres is a limited partnership open only to accredited investors. (See cerespartners.com to obtain a private placement memorandum.) There are also plentiful opportunities to invest in farmland in Canada and other non-U.S. countries. See the section, "Become a Foreign Farmer," in Chapter 8.

Risks of Farmland Investing

If you invest in farmland, know what you're getting into. A farmland investment is illiquid and subject to supply and demand imbalances that can depress commodity prices. Drought, weather, and disease can damage crops, with permanent crops like citrus trees being especially vulnerable. Many opportunities to buy farmland are not publicly traded or subject to audit by outside advisors. Tread carefully and perform a reasonable investigation into what you are buying into.

Farmland prices in the U.S. Midwest are up 32.5 percent from 2010, the biggest annual increase in the 70 years surveyed. Some economists worry that the market has become overheated, setting the stage for a farmland bust.[13]

Investment newsletter author Gonzalo Lira points out further risks that will become operative in a hyperinflation environment.[14] Farms are highly dependent on credit to buy feed and equipment. If interest rates become exorbitantly high, many farms will fail.

Farmers may also simply choose not to plant crops during an era of rapidly rising expenses for fear that they can't afford production and/or harvesting costs. This suggests that while farmland may act as an inflation hedge during periods of "normal" inflation, prices may crash during periods of hyperinflation for all but the best financed and managed farms.

Key Points

- Housing prices have returned to their prebubble trend line, signaling that the worst is over in the real estate market.
- Take advantage of historic low interest rates, and drive a hard bargain for some foreclosed property.
- In some areas it's cheaper to own than rent.
- Owning apartment buildings is a business that can provide long-term cash flow.
- Avoid buying income property in rent-controlled areas.
- U.S. farmland prices have been heading up, providing opportunities for patient investors.
- As a hedge, farmland investing may work best in periods of relatively steady inflation.

CHAPTER

4

Dollar Down = Oil Up

America's appetite for oil puts it on a collision course with world events. The rising consumption of India and China and likely increases in demand as the globe moves out of the Great Recession means higher prices—a trend exacerbated by the predicted decline of "peak oil." As other countries perceive weakness in the dollar, a move is afoot to set oil loose from its dollar moorings, meaning further price hikes. Investors can hedge against dollar decline by investing in oil exchange-traded funds (ETFs), stocks of major oil companies, or shares of supply-chain related industries.

Why You Need to Invest in Black Gold

In March 2003, the price of a barrel of oil was $26. Five years later, it had risen to $100 per barrel, and a few months later hit a high of $147 a barrel. Trillions of dollars from the United States, Asia, and Europe flooded into Middle Eastern countries over the next year, exacerbating the international recession that had started with the U.S. housing meltdown.

Currently, the United States consumes over 20 million barrels of oil every day, about one-quarter of the world's demand. While prices fell as low as $40 per barrel in response to the recession, pent-up demand remains and prices in December 2011 hovered around the $100 mark.[1] Repeated policy initiatives by the Obama administration to "invest" in renewable energy are unlikely to have much effect on America's growing appetite for oil as renewable sources have not proven to be economically viable.

Furthermore, as other countries perceive the folly of America's spending spree and the consequent weakening of the U.S. dollar, there is a movement to end dollar dealings for oil. Instead, if China, Russia, France, and the Gulf Arabs get their way, oil will be priced in the euro, the yuan, and gold by 2018—a drastic blow to American economic power. *Bloomberg Businessweek* reports that secret meetings have already been held to such an end by central bankers and finance ministers of those countries.[2]

Consequently, as the recession eases and other nations seek to flee the weakening U.S. dollar, the price of oil in U.S. dollars will rise—slowly at first, as central bankers divest themselves of dollar reserves, then much more rapidly.

Why Proved Reserve Figures Are Unreliable

Proved reserves are the quantity of crude oil estimated to be in place and recoverable under existing conditions. Not all the oil in place in an oil field is recoverable because of geologic conditions, and there is no international authority that audits claims of reserves. For political or economic purposes, some national governments exaggerate their estimates of oil reserves.

OPEC establishes market prices as a percentage of stated reserves, creating an incentive for members to publicly overestimate reserves in order to be able to sell more oil now, today, to prop up current regimes.

Saudi Reserves Overstated?

Diplomatic cables released by WikiLeaks in February 2011 indicate that Saudi Arabia may have overstated its reserves by nearly 40 percent.[3] The Saudis are a major tempering force in OPEC, often raising oil production to offset threatened price increases.

The obvious downside of overstated reserves is that, at some point, reality will collide with estimates. As those proved reserves disappear in a puff of accounting smoke and mirrors, the laws of supply and demand will push oil prices up.

Is the World Running Out of Oil?

While changing methods of oil recovery can make previously unrecoverable oil recoverable, such methods can be enormously expensive and only sustainable if the price of oil is high. For this reason, some suspect that the production of oil has peaked or will peak sometime in the next decades. M. King Hubbert created models that accurately predicted that U.S. oil production would peak between 1965 and 1970.[4] The same Hubbert curve shows world oil production peaking between 2000 and 2005 (see Figure 4.1).

The Hubbert curve predicts that we are at or near the peak of oil production. A little-known 2009 Department of Energy report, "Report on the Risks and Impacts of a Potential Future Decline in Oil Production,"[5] offers a range of estimates on the timing of the peak; see Figure 4.2.

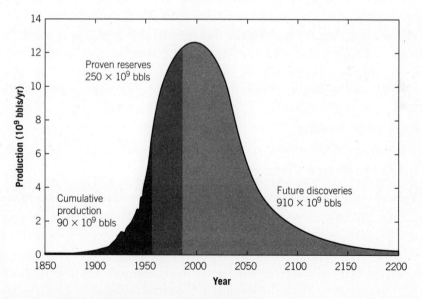

Figure 4.1   Hubbert's 1956 Projection of Peak Oil Production

Source: M. King, Hubbert, "Nuclear Energy and the Fossil Fuels," Publication no. 95., (Houston: Shell Development Company, 1956).

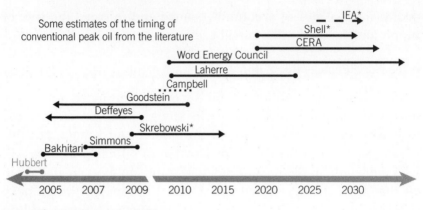

Figure 4.2   Countdown to Peak Oil?

Source: "Report on the Risks and Impacts of a Potential Future Decline in Oil Production," Rep. no. 11D/707 (Washington D.C.: Department of Energy & Climate Change, 2009).

While the world is not in any danger of "running out" of oil anytime in this century (indeed, oil is being produced at near record volumes), the rate of production is beginning to decline.

The collision between increasing world demand and declining world supply is yet another indicator of much higher oil prices in the near future. Right now the worldwide recession is creating a glut of supply for weakened industries. But factor in the dollar's increasing weakness and the threat of war in the Middle East, and oil analyst Charles T. Maxwell sees crude oil at $300 per barrel by 2020. According to Maxwell, "The world simply won't have enough oil to meet demand."[6]

Will Abiotic Oil Avert a Hubbert Curve Peak?

The Hubbert curve rests on an assumption that some scientists are beginning to question: that oil is a fossil fuel, created over the eons by the decay of ancient life. An alternative hypothesis of petroleum's origins—that oil is forming continuously from deep hydrocarbon deposits in the earth, transformed by thermophilic bacteria and welling up near the surface—gained popularity in Russia and the Ukraine in the 1950s and 1960s and was popularized by the publication in 1998 of "The Deep Hot Biosphere," by

National Academy of Sciences member and Cornell University professor Thomas Gold.

Gold convinced the Swedish State Power Board to drill for oil in nonsedimentary rock that had been fractured by a meteorite—rock that shouldn't have contained oil. It did, lending support to the abiotic hypothesis.[7] If the abiotic theory is correct, estimates of how much oil remains to be exploited will have to be revised drastically upward. Instead of peak oil, suggests Daniel Yergin, chairman of IHS Cambridge Energy Research Associates, we may enter a period of "plateau oil," with supplies of oil gradually flattening out toward midcentury.[8]

But even if the supply of oil plateaus instead of declining, voracious world demand for energy will continue to push prices up. The United States, China, Japan, and India are all expected to use dramatically more oil in the coming two decades, pointing to a continued upward pressure on oil prices.[9]

Political and Environmental Pressures Are Pushing Oil Prices Up

As the dollar collapses under the weight of unsustainable government spending, expect the price of oil to move decisively—and explosively—upward. A signal for that movement will be any political instability in the Arabian Peninsula, especially a war involving Israel and Iran or other Arab states.

Short of war, continuing political problems in Libya, Iraq, Iran, and other oil-producing countries of the Middle East are likely to create production shortfalls that will drive oil prices up, according to a report issued by the International Energy Agency (IEA).

"There is a possibility that production growth from the Middle East and North Africa . . . may not be what consumers would like to see," commented IEA economist Fatih Birol, adding, "This would be a pity for the global economy."[10]

Add to this the aftereffects of the disastrous BP oil spill in the Gulf of Mexico, which put a squeeze on supplies in several ways. First, the administration put a six-month moratorium on deep water drilling permits in the gulf, which put over 20 billion barrels of oil off limits (over three-quarters of proven U.S. reserves).

Second, the administration has made it increasingly difficult to obtain drilling permits and meet regulatory burdens, as government overseers clamp down on potentially risky drilling practices. Recent announcements of "new" permits seem to be designed to placate environmentalists while continuing to halt Gulf oil production.[11]

Shale Gas—Energy Bright Spot?

Shale gas production in the United States has rocketed from zero a decade ago to about 30 percent of the country's natural gas supply due to new geological insights and hydraulic fracturing ("fracking") technology.[12] Shale gas is a cleaner substitute for coal in firing electrical generators, but fracking is bitterly opposed by some environmentalists, who fear contamination of water supplies:

"With hydrofracking, a well can produce over a million gallons of wastewater that is often laced with highly corrosive salts, carcinogens like benzene and radioactive elements like radium, all of which can occur naturally thousands of feet underground," says a paper cited by the *New York Times.*[13]

Nonetheless, shale gas seems destined to play a bigger role in the U.S. energy mix over the coming decades as environmentally safer methods are developed to extract the resource and environmentalists and industry come to terms on drilling regulations.

Halliburton (symbol: HAL), for instance, is working on fracking fluids that are environmentally benign.[14] Carbo Ceramics (symbol: CRR) supplies a ceramic product that helps keep gas flowing by holding fractured rocks apart.[15] Other shale gas players include Devon Energy (symbol: DVN), which first applied horizontal drilling to shale gas formations; Cabot Oil & Gas (symbol: COG), which holds interest from Appalacia to Texas to Canada; Anadarko Petroleum (symbol: APC); and Baker Hughes (symbol: BHI).

The World's Biggest Oil Companies and Their Ticker Symbols

Whatever the future brings in regards to oil production, it's pretty certain that the world's biggest private oil companies will be on top of it. Table 4.1 lists a few stocks you might want to investigate for your portfolio.

Table 4.1   The Top 10 Privately Traded Oil Companies

Company	Symbol	Market Cap ($ billion)
ExxonMobil	XOM	$406.3
PetroChina Company Limited	PTR	$276.6
Royal Dutch Shell	RDSA	$234.6
Chevron Corporation	CVX	$211.9
Petroleo Brasileiro S.A.	PBR	$156.3
BP	BP	$135.5
Gazprom	GZPFY	$122.6
Total S.A.	TOT	$121.0
China Petroleum & Chemical Corp.	SNP	$ 97.4
ConocoPhillips	COP	$ 96.8 (as of 12/31/11)

Source: PFC Energy.

The Easy Way to Own Oil

You can invest in oil directly on the commodities market, but trading commodities is a very volatile and highly leveraged operation that requires constant supervision of trades and plenty of expertise. A much easier way to own petroleum is through petroleum ETFs, similar to the ETFs already discussed for gold and silver. Unlike the gold and silver ETFs, the oil ETFs own a basket of commodity contracts for the delivery of oil, not physical oil. This does increase your exposure to financial meltdowns or incompetent management (or fraud), but for all but the most sophisticated investors, the relative convenience outweighs risks.

Two ETFs to look into are the United States 12 Month Oil Fund (symbol: USL) and the United States Oil Fund (USO). Each ETF uses future contracts to approximate price movements of light, sweet crude oil (West Texas Intermediate or WTI).

How to Profit from the Oil Supply Chain

Demand for oil goes down in a recession. That eases prices. The demand for oil can swing wildly from year to year or month to month in response to economic conditions.

But what about the supply side of the equation? Discovering oil, drilling for it, building pipelines, transporting oil, refining oil, and distributing oil—all that takes time. So supply is inelastic, meaning it can't bounce all over the place.

Put the two sides of the equation together and what do you find? That stocks in drilling companies, pipeline companies, tanker companies, and refineries get beaten down badly when lack of demand drives prices to $60 per barrel. But as soon as demand begins to perk up, these companies revive, big time. Deep sea drillers are booked months in advance, pipe and oil equipment producers can't keep up with the business, and there is a shortage of refining capacity.

These companies are poised to win big from the supply bottleneck that inevitably develops when demand for oil bounces back. The world runs on oil, whether paid for in U.S. dollars or not.

Some oil supply chain stocks worth watching: ENSCO (symbol: ESV), which contracts offshore drilling; Schlumberger (symbol: SLB), a huge and wide-ranging oilfield services company, and National Oilwell Varco (symbol: NOV), which also provides oilfield inspection services.

Should I Invest in Oil Drilling?

Investments in oil and gas drilling take many forms, including limited partnerships, ownership of fractional undivided interest in leases, and general partnerships. In other words, if you invest in these ways, you are becoming part-owner of an oil drilling business.

Would you go into the dry cleaning business without substantial knowledge of the operation of such a business, its prospects of success, and the monetary risks you run?

If you have such knowledge, by all means consider investing in oil drilling partnerships. If not, beware of boiler room and Internet pitches claiming that risks of investing in oil drilling partnerships are minimal or that "a geologist" has confidence the well will produce.

Avoiding Oil Investment Scams

Scams in oil drilling companies are notorious—so much so that the Securities and Exchange Commission has created a special Web page devoted to red flags: http://www.sec.gov/investor/pubs/oilgasscams.htm.

There are many legitimate oil and gas drilling investments out there, but such ventures are speculative. Like all speculative investments, only invest if you want to take a gamble and can stand to lose the money.

Canadian Royalty Trusts: Good Investments No Longer

Canadian royalty trusts ("CanRoys") are oil and natural gas producers that in the past typically paid high dividends. Unlike U.S. royalty trusts, Canadian royalty trusts are allowed to acquire new oil and gas properties as existing properties are depleted. Thus, dividends from U.S. royalty trusts decline over time, while Canadian trusts can bring new properties online and operate indefinitely.

CanRoys were a favorite of international investors seeking sustained high dividends, but all that changed during the 2007 "Halloween massacre"—Ottawa's decision to tax trusts in the same manner as corporations, phasing out CanRoys' tax advantages by 2011.[16] Upon the announcement, CanRoy stocks immediately plummeted, and some 90 percent of CanRoys have since converted to corporations.[17]

Key Points

- The U.S. economy runs on oil, consuming about one-quarter of the world's production.
- Increasing demand from China and the developing world will put upward pressure on oil prices, as will the economic uptick as the world economy recovers.
- Some scientists theorize that the world may be reaching peak oil production and the beginning of a long decline. Reserves may be overstated as well.
- The development of shale gas through fracking may relieve some U.S. dependence on foreign oil.
- ETFs offer a direct way to invest in oil.
- Shares of major oil companies and oil field suppliers are closely linked to oil prices.
- Avoid oil drilling partnerships and Canadian CanRoys.

CHAPTER 5

From Diamonds to Trees: Alternative Assets

Gold, silver, and oil are good investments to protect your wealth from inflation because of their widespread acceptance, easy liquidity, and recognized value. In the interest of hedging your portfolio even further, however, you may wish to dabble with a small percentage of your money in other tangible assets such as stamps, art, or diamonds.

Another Precious Metal—Platinum

Platinum, one of the rarest metals on earth, is another precious metal sometimes traded for investment value.

Platinum's value comes mainly from its utility to industry, so, unlike gold, there are few speculative forces affecting its value. Platinum is a key component, for instance, in your car's catalytic converter, and has other significant uses in the electronics and chemical industries.[1]

For the same reason, however, platinum's cost rises and falls with the world economy and is thus significantly more volatile than gold. At the onset of the worldwide recession in 2008, for instance, platinum's price plunged from around $2,200 to $775 per ounce, while gold dropped only about 30 percent. Platinum was trading at the end of 2011 at just above $1,500 per ounce.

Platinum, like gold, can be acquired in a variety of ways. Platinum coins (the Platinum Australian Koala, the Platinum Canadian Maple Leaf, and the Platinum American Eagle) can be purchased through the same coin and precious metal dealers who deal in gold and silver. Several exchange-traded funds (ETFs) are devoted to platinum: ETFS Physical Platinum Shares (symbol: PHPT) are invested in physical platinum and thus directly correlate to the metal's price. E-TRACS Long Platinum ETN is linked to the platinum futures index and offers indirect exposure, but carries with it the inherent risk of all ETNs, as previously discussed.

Platinum's supply situation is tight. South Africa supplies 60 percent of the world's production, and *Barron*'s commentator Tatyana Shumsky points out that "platinum mines are the deepest and most dangerous in the world."[2] If mining ceased today, the world's supply would be exhausted in a single year.[3]

In sum: Platinum is a precious metal whose fortunes are tied closely to the health of the industrial economy. Its value will rise and fall with the economic winds, but in the long run it will prove a better store of value than the U.S. dollar.

Why You Should Stay Away from Palladium

Palladium, which in 2011 traded in the $550 to $850 per ounce range, has also recently become available as ETFs and as palladium coins. However, buying palladium involves an unknown risk: a huge Russian government stockpile from the Soviet era.

"No one really knows how much palladium Russia has," says Robin Bhar, metal analyst for Credit Agricole. "It's a state secret."[4]

Approximately 18 million ounces of palladium were sold from the Russian stockpiles between 1993 and 2001, but now Russia's Norilsk Nickel, the world's largest palladium producer, has stated it will sharply cut sales from the stockpile over the next two years.[5]

Tightened supplies will raise the price—but is the shortfall of palladium real or artificial? No one knows, but the palladium "shortfall" is as likely to be due to price manipulation as real demand shortage. Palladium is therefore a speculative investment not suitable as a hedge against a falling dollar.

What about Stamps?

Stamp collecting makes sense as a hobby, but how does it fare as an investment? A study by Elroy Dimson of the London Business School and Cristophe Spaenjens of Tilburg University concludes that over the last century stamps provided an annualized return of 7 percent in nominal terms (2.9 percent in real terms). Not great, but better than bonds over the same period.

What's more, in times of economic upheaval, investors fleeing from currency tend to run up the price of stamps. Investment grade stamps rose 35 percent in 2008. The authors' conclusion: "Stamps and other real assets... appear to thrive in highly inflationary environments. . . . Stamps hedge against expected inflation."[6] (See Figure 5.1.)

Stanley Gibbons, the oldest and most reputable stamp dealer in the world, offers a number of investment plans. In the Capital Protected Growth Plan, for instance, investors buy a set amount of rare stamps, which are held by the company in its vaults. After five years, investors can take possession of the stamps or they can be sold at auction. Thirty percent of the profits go to Gibbons, which,

Figure 5.1   These Two Penny Blues Sold for over £200,000 at Auction

however, guarantees the investor against any losses should the market dip.[7] The minimum investment is £10,000.

Getting Started In Stamps

If stamps pique your interest, the Dimson-Spaenjers study will give you a head start on understanding the market. It's called, "Ex Post: The Investment Performance of Collectible Stamps." Find it online at http://papers.ssrn.com.

The Danger of Diamonds

Like gold, diamonds are an almost irresistible form of wealth. They are portable, tangible, and private, in addition to being beautiful and useful. Diamond value, though, is contingent on their rarity, which is open to manipulation and changes as new diamond sources are discovered and old ones are mined out.

Two companies, De Beers and Alrosa, together control about 95 percent of the diamond market. They have been under antitrust pressure by the European High Court, which in 2010 annulled a sales agreement between the two companies.[8, 9]

Like other markets, the diamond market has been reacting to anticipated weakening of the dollar with rising prices. India and China have emerged as big diamond consumers, contributing to 20 percent of the global demand in 2011.[10] Demand for big stones has been consistently growing, driven by fashion trends in jewelry and investor worry.

Says Laurence Graff, head of London-based Graff Diamonds, "When people worry that their dollars are worth nothing, they want assets that will increase in value—silent assets that you can put in your pocket because tomorrow, anything can go wrong."[11]

Be that as it may, supply and demand in the diamond industry is tightly controlled by a few key players. Polished white diamonds, most traded by investors, serve as pricing benchmarks in this field, but even Sotheby's cautions against trading in these gems for investment purposes.[12] Not only is the market subject to manipulation, but because every diamond is different and cut and clarity affect value, it can be difficult to sell diamonds when you want to.

Diamonds as jewelry, yes. As a hedge against inflation? There are better choices.

Art: Love It or Leave It

Buying and selling fine art is not for the faint hearted, as artists go in and out of favor and the price of art is highly volatile. When the economy is going well, art tends to underperform, but, like stamps, art takes off in times of uncertainty.

The investment art market is fragmented into different sectors that rise and fall with trends in taste. For instance, in 2010 prices of Old Masters increased by 17 percent while American works created before 1950 declined by 30 percent.[13] Sales of art at auction slowed dramatically at the height of the recession, but in 2010 began to recover.

According to Michael Moses, co-creator of the Mei Moses All Art Index, the art market tends to trail the stock market by six to 18 months.[14] (That widely followed index is based on a proprietary database of over 13,000 purchases over the last 15 years.[15]) Such lags suggest that the art market is illiquid and requires patience. Overall, art as an investment tends to appreciate at a rate of about 10.5 percent, according to research by New York University Stern School of Business—compared to 10.9 percent for the S&P 500 index.[16]

If you are interested in investing in art, spend a lot of time visiting galleries and museums. Decide on a specialty you like and deal with the most reputable dealers in that specialty. Buy and sell as markets rise and fall and as your taste changes. Don't buy anything you don't love, because you may be staring at it for a long time.

How to Get Money to Grow on Trees

Investing in timber may not be glamorous, but it definitely can be profitable. Since 1987, for instance, managed timber produced a return of 15 percent, compared to 9.6 percent for the stock market.[17] Timber is a dull investment, with little volatility, but performs especially well in bear markets (timber went up 233 percent during the Great Depression, while the price of stocks nose-dived 70 percent).[18]

Moreover, timber proved to be an excellent hedge during the inflationary 1970s. While annual inflation averaged 9.2 percent from 1973 to 1981, timberland holdings went up an average of 22 percent.[19] And since 1980, global trade of forest products has grown at a robust 4.4 percent annual average growth rate. (See Figure 5.2.)

With China and India ramping up manufacturing, demand for wood will double by the year 2050, according to the Food and Agricultural Organization of the United Nations.[20] Big insurance companies and pension funds have been investing in timber for the last 20 years, and a recent study showed that a timber portfolio would have returned 13.3 percent annually over the past four decades—compared with 11.6 percent for the S&P 500.[21, 22] (See Figure 5.3.)

And—unlike other commodities—trees grow, an average of about 8 percent a year.[23] And larger trees are more valuable. A cord

Figure 5.2   Demand for Wood Products Continues to Grow: Global Trade of Forest Products, 1980–2010

Source: Food and Agricultural Organization of the United Nations (FAOSTAT); Chart: Wood Resource International LLC.

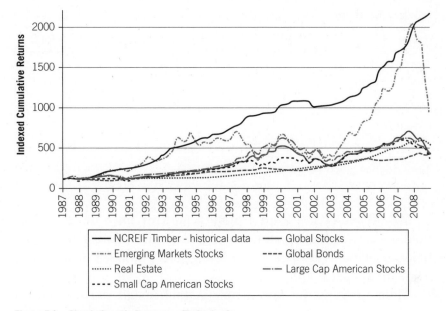

Figure 5.3   Steady Growth: Returns on Timberlands

Source: "Timberland Investments in an Institutional Portfolio," (report) International Woodland.

of Southern Pine from 12-year-old trees sells for about $20. At twice that age, the price triples to $60—a winner any way you cut it.[24]

Don't Knock Wood

"A cord of Southern Pine from 12-year-old trees sells for about $20. At twice that age, the price triples to $60—a winner any way you cut it."

Some 70 percent of timberland in North America is privately owned. Individuals with $1 million and up to invest should investigate Timberland Investment Management Organizations (TIMOs), which acts as a broker between timberland owners and large investors.

If you're not in a position to make a seven-figure investment, you can buy stock in public companies that own huge acreages of managed timber. Table 5.1 gives some suggestions.

Table 5.1   Timber Plays

Company	Symbol	Acres of Timber (Millions)	Recent Price ($U.S.)
Weyerhaeuser	WY	22.0	17.23
Plum Creek Timber	PCL	7.0	35.99
Rayonier	RYN	2.5	41.50
Potlatch Corp.	PCH	1.7	30.72
Deltic Timber	DEL	0.4	43.99

Source: Company reports.

Weyerhaeuser has been a public company since the 1960s. Its holdings are of high-quality timber, which ties its fortunes to the housing market (as opposed to lower-quality wood, which can be made into paper pulp.)

Plum Creek is the purest play in timber and prides itself on its advanced silviculture practices, which improve the productivity of its forests. It owns timberlands in more than a dozen American states and is the largest private landowner in the nation.

Rayonier Inc. owns timberland in both the United States and New Zealand and holds non-timber-related real estate, which somewhat dilutes its value as a timber play.

Potlatch Industries is a vertically integrated company that engages not only in timber sales but in lumber, pulp manufacturing, and consumer products.[25] That helps even out swings in earnings but, again, dilutes its value as a timber play.

Deltic Timber, the smallest company, is in some ways the most interesting. Deltic owns 437,700 acres of Arkansas timberland (mostly Southern Pine), which it cuts and manages on a 35-year cycle (as opposed to an industry-norm 20-year cycle). Most of its land sits over the Fayetteville Shale formation, which may have hidden natural gas potential.[26]

In the last decade, Weyerhaeuser, Plum Creek, Rayonier, and Potlatch have restructured themselves as real-estate investment trusts (REITS), which pay little or no tax because REITs can deduct shareholder dividends from corporate taxable income, allowing them to apply more capital toward land acquisition.[27]

Finally, as with gold and silver, you can now invest in timber ETFs. The Guggenheim Timber Index (symbol: CUT) invests in stocks and other financial instruments that correlate to the Beacon Global Timber Index, which tracks prices of forest land, lumber, pulp, and paper. Another ETF choice is the iShares S&P Global Timber & Forestry Index Fund (symbol: WOOD), which consists of publicly traded companies in the forest products supply chain.

But approach timber ETFs with caution. At least one analyst, George Nichols, calls timber ETFs "a sector bet disguised as an 'asset class'" bet—meaning the performance of the timber ETFs may have more to do with the construction sector of the economy than with the underlying asset price of timber.

Profit Opportunity: People Have to Eat

Inflation has already started in your local grocery store, where surging farm prices have driven U.S. food costs up a sharp 4 percent in 2011 (from 0.8 percent the year before), according to the U.S. Department of Agriculture. Eggs, meat, fruits, and vegetables all are more costly, driven by high Chinese demand for soybeans and the increasing use of corn to create biofuels. Global prices were up even more—some 25 percent—as world grain inventories declined.[28, 29, 30]

With high unemployment lingering, shoppers responded to the price increases by cutting back on their purchases or trading down to cheaper products. The Frugal Dad blog, for instance, recommends swapping beans for meats, eating more leftovers, and setting up a home vegetable garden. One respondent commented, "We keep our portions a lot smaller these days and I use half the amount of meat I used to."[31]

Still, people have to eat, and food costs often rise precipitously when inflation goes hyper. In the former Soviet republic of Belarus, as inflation rates reached 50 percent in 2011, foodstuffs began to disappear from shelves.[32] "All meat has gone to Russia," a tractor plant worker said. "My relatives near the Russian border called me a few days ago and said the shops are empty."[33]

General Mills (stock symbol: GIS), Kellogg (K), Nestle (NSRGY .PK), Heinz (HNZ), and Kraft (KFT) all are trusted brands with worldwide diversification and should have the pricing power to pass along commodity price increases to consumers.

A commodity-related agricultural play for U.S. markets is the PowerShares DB Agriculture Fund ETF (symbol: DBA). It invests in corn, wheat, soybeans, and sugar.

Another portfolio possibility: investment in companies like Monsanto (symbol: MON), or Terra Nitrogen (symbol: TNH) and Potash (symbol: POT). These seed and fertilizer companies will benefit from rising food prices without being hurt by rising energy and production costs.

The Copper Shortfall

Copper is a critical industrial commodity that is projected to see shortfalls in 2012 for the third straight year. Copper is widely used in wire, piping, communications, electrical distribution, and electronics. Demand for the metal has remained healthy despite the recession, and China, the world's biggest consumer, is expected to increase demand another 6 percent in 2012. Worldwide, demand in 2011 exceeded supply by almost a half-million metric tons, and copper reached a record price of $10,190 a ton in February 2011 (see Figure 5.4).[34]

In the United States, skyrocketing copper prices have even created a burgeoning industry of copper thieves, who are costing construction and industrial sites an estimated $1 billion a year in theft damage.[35]

The explosion of ETFs has created a way for the average investor to invest in this industrial metal without buying huge quantities.

The United States Copper Index Fund (symbol: CPER) is structured as a publicly-traded limited partnership. Although it does not physically hold a reserve of copper metal (as, say, the gold ETFs GLD and IAU do), it seeks to mitigate credit market risks

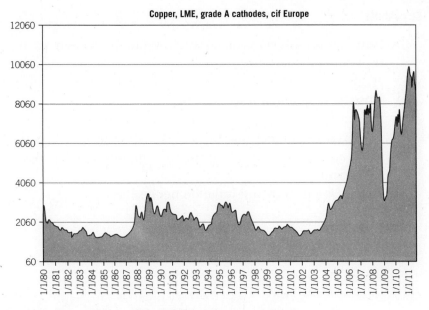

Figure 5.4   Price of Copper, 1980–2010 (U.S. dollars per metric ton)
Source: Mongabay.com.

by collateralizing copper future contracts with three-month U.S. Treasury Bills.

The First Trust ISE Global Copper Index Fund (symbol: CU) invests in copper mining and related stocks. Some of the companies in its portfolio, however, may engage in mining and processing other metals such as gold and silver, thus diluting the fund as a pure copper play. The Global X Copper Miners ETF (symbol: COPX) also invests in equities of companies in the global copper mining industry.

There are also two exchange-traded note (ETN) vehicles (not recommended as a hedge for reasons previously discussed). The iPath Dow Jones-UBS Total Return ETN (symbol: JJC) and the iPath Pure Beta Copper ETN (symbol: CUPM) are ETN products tied to various futures trading strategies involving the metal. In addition to the risks inherent in all ETNs, these carry exposure risks to the futures market.[36] Use caution.

Key Points

- Platinum is a precious metal with a value that closely mirrors the economic outlook.
- Huge Russian stockpiles of palladium make its price subject to market manipulation.
- Two cartels control 95 percent of the diamond market, leaving investors at their mercy.
- Both art and stamps perform well in times of economic uncertainty.
- Timber is a proven anti-inflation hedge.

Future Money Is Cheap Money

Our second general principle to preserve your money against the coming government inflation: Avoid adjustable-rate loans and push paying back other fixed obligations into the far future.

Adjustable-rate loans are any loans where the interest rate changes—adjusts—from time to time. Typically adjustments on such loans are triggered by changes in an agreed-upon index, such as the LIBOR (London Interbank Offered Rate). Adjustable-rate loans may seem attractive because of low initial interest rates, but they are time bombs waiting to go off. That's because any underlying index is bound to rise as inflation rises. And then your interest rate—and payments—will skyrocket.

Adjustable-rate loans are your enemy in an inflationary environment. Fixed-rate loans are your friends. (That's why the bankers make it easier for you to get into adjustable-rate loans. You take the risk—not them.) If you use other fixed obligations—for instance, a balloon note to pay for a business you're buying—it's to your advantage in an inflationary environment to push back that payment as far as possible. That way you're paying a loan obtained today with cheapened, devalued money caused by future inflation. That $1,000 obligation won't seem so daunting when inflation makes a pound of coffee cost $100.

CHAPTER

Beat the Banks at Their Own Game

Banks stack the deck when it comes to issuing loans and investing your money. But by anticipating a high rate of inflation, you can push some risk back onto the financial institutions. Today's fixed-rate mortgages—held at artificially low rates by the Federal Reserve—will prove a long-term bargain as inflation erodes the value of your payments. But high rates of inflation will also come with political risks. Access to your accounts may be impaired and FDIC "insurance" may prove illusory.

Why Fixed-Rate Mortgages Are Your Friend

In the coming government inflation-storm, a fixed-rate mortgage will make you smile. That's because in a fixed-rate mortgage, the lender will be absorbing the cost of inflation.

Currently, 30-year fixed-rate mortgage interest rates are at historic lows. The bankers seem to be betting that inflation over the next 30 years will be relatively mild. You, of course, should be betting the other way. Here's why: Assume you finance a $300,000 home loan at a rate of 4.5 percent. Your monthly payments will be approximately $1,064. Assume, for the sake of argument, that inflation averages 8 percent per year for the next 10 years. In 10 years, your payment will still be $1,064. But $1,064 in 10 years will, after inflation, only buy what you could buy for $462 today. In other words, inflation forced your banker to eat $602—the value of lost purchasing power.

Take a Cue from Your Parents

"If you have a fixed-rate loan, inflation works in your favor even if you never save a cent. . . . That's why Mom and Dad's home loan payments always seem so laughably small."

If you have a fixed-rate loan, inflation works in your favor even if you never save a cent. That's because your wages will likely rise with the rate of inflation. The $20 per hour you get today will magically turn into $43.18 10 years from now. To be clear, $43.18 10 years from now will only buy the same amount of goods that $20 will buy today.

But—and this is a big but—your banker is still getting paid the same dollar payment that he did at the start of the loan. You're paying him with cheapened dollars. That's why Mom and Dad's home loan payments always seem so laughably small.

Moral: Don't fall for adjustable-rate home mortgages. Make sure all of your properties have fixed-rate loans at the lowest interest rate you can find.

Cut Your Mortgage in Half

If you really want to make your banker sick, cut your mortgage in half by accelerating your payments.

Because of the way home loans are structured, in the early years of your mortgage, the bulk of your payment is going to pay interest, with only a small percentage actually paying down the principal of your loan. For instance, on a $300,000 loan at 4.5 percent interest, the first loan payment is $1,520. Of that, only $395 goes toward principal; the rest is interest.

Some banks offer—for a fee—a bimonthly payment schedule, which would in fact knock five years off the loan just discussed. But you can do better yourself. When you write your mortgage check, simply include a second check for the amount of the principal as a "principal only" payment. In the example above, you would write an additional check for $395.

Those additional small principal payments will actually pay your mortgage off in *half* the normal time. Looked at another way, that $395 paid today is knocking your next month's payment from your mortgage, saving you $1,125—the balance of the payment you would otherwise have to make.[1]

Note, however, that if you are a very disciplined investor, you may be able to find better places to invest that $395. Says Laura Rowley at Yahoo! Finance,

> Using very conservative figures, investing instead of prepaying the mortgage yields an extra $400 per year. If you feel compelled to pay down your mortgage, do it. But realize you're paying a price to do so.[2]

For many people—especially if you would squander that extra payment rather than invest it—the certainty of getting the bank off their back early is worth forgoing any theoretical future investment income.

Don't Get Locked into HELOCs

During the housing boom, a lot of us took a home equity loan against the rising value of our house. And why not? Prices were appreciating so fast that our equity was ballooning. We wanted to use some of that equity to start a business, remodel the basement, or pay for that plastic surgery.

That was then. This is now. Don't expect home prices to roar upward over the next decade as the economy limps along under a huge tax burden and government-induced superinflation.

Because a HELOC (Home Equity Line of Credit) is generally an adjustable-rate loan, you can plan on the interest rate going up as prices start to rise. HELOCs are usually based on the prime rate, plus or minus a margin. The prime rate is currently the lowest it has been in years, but this won't last as superinflation kicks in. Then you, not the banks, are exposed to interest rate risks.

Get out of your HELOC. Act now to take advantage of low prime interest rates and refinance to a fixed-rate second mortgage (or roll your HELOC into a refinance of your first mortgage).

Buy Big Houses and Lease Used Cars

Over the long term, houses tend to appreciate in value, while cars depreciate. And new cars depreciate fastest of all.

Car loans, like home loans, used to be straightforward fixed-rate loans, usually of a period of three to five years. To make payments lower, lately car makers have been stretching out the loans to six or even seven years, and have introduced HELOC-like variable-rate interest loans.

Although there is a delicate dance between the resale value of your car and the balance due on your loan, one thing is for certain: A variable-rate auto loan dumps the risk of inflation onto you.

So don't finance a car with a variable-rate loan, no matter how low the initial interest rate seems. Otherwise, your car payments will heat up right alongside inflation. Stick with a conventional fixed-rate auto loan or a guaranteed lease payment.

One other factor to consider in an inflationary environment is the length of your car loan. Ordinarily, stretching car payments out to five, six, or even seven years almost guarantees that at some point your car will be worth less than the balance you owe on your loan. Not normally a good idea.

But what if inflation takes a big leap? You will be paying for your car—a tangible asset with a definite utilitarian value—with dollars that have been cheapened, effectively getting a discount on your loan.

Is that a wise move? Difficult to calculate, as the declining (real) value of your particular vehicle has to be measured against the inflation-discounted value of your car payment. There are so many variables here that it's probably better to play it safe and stick with shorter-length car loans. That way you win no matter what happens to the inflation rate.

If Your House Is in Foreclosure

If your house is in foreclosure, you are not alone.

1.4 million homes nationwide—3.4 percent of homes with mortgages—were in foreclosure at the end of 2011, and over 7 percent of homeowners are 90 days or more late in their payments.[3] After a slight decrease in 2011, foreclosure filings began ticking up again 3 percent in January 2012.[4] The 2009 Homeowner Affordability and Stability Plan (HAMP) provided help to only 13 percent of underwater homeowners in 2011.[5] Since its inception, some 640,000 people have benefited from HAMP—not the four million the president said the program would help.[6] And the robo-signing settlement negotiated by the attorneys general of many states was even less generous, amounting to $213 per potentially affected homeowner.[7]

If you're behind on your payments, you may be able to negotiate a repayment plan, forbearance, or modification with your lender. To start, get in touch with the workout or loan modification department and file the paperwork for the modification. Lenders generally require a hardship letter explaining how you got into a financial jam and detailed information about your finances, including bank account statements and income tax forms. Be aware that the process typically takes months, and may or may not end in a successful restructuring of your loan.[8]

Delay tactics can buy you time to catch up with your payments. You can challenge the validity of a foreclosure sale, asking the trustee to determine that all the legal i's have been dotted and t's crossed in the lender's foreclosure filing. The trustee will delay the sale until these points have been resolved. Another tactic that has proved successful in a number of cases is demanding that the bank produce the note that proves they are the legal holder of the mortgage—a paperwork burden the bank may not be able to bear, since your original mortgage may have been traded several times between different banking institutions. Finally, filing for bankruptcy will cause the court to freeze all your bills. You may be able to use the leverage of the bankruptcy process to renegotiate your mortgage, reaffirming the debt with court approval.[9]

If your goal is simply to get out from under the burden of your payments, you may be able to effect a short sale, in which, with the agreement of the lending bank, the house is sold for less than the balance of the mortgage. The short sale will generally be recorded on your credit report as "paid in full for less than agreed" and stays on the record for seven years. The real danger of a short sale, however, is that that in some states the lender may come after you for a deficiency judgment—the deficiency being the difference between the balance owed and the amount of the sale. (An attorney may be able to negotiate away this danger as part of the short sale agreement.) Finally, be aware that beginning in 2013, the IRS may consider the amount of the forbearance taxable income.[10]

A Customer Service Secret

The toll-free phone number on the back of your credit card generally connects with call centers in India, the Philippines, or other overseas locations. If you want to speak to a representative based in the United States, call in on the "international call collect" number. Though not toll free, this number will connect you to a United States–based service rep more likely to have authority to resolve your banking issues.[11]

FDIC "Insurance" May Be Hazardous to Your Wealth

Although bank accounts are insured up to $250,000 per depositor per bank by the Federal Deposit Insurance Corporation (FDIC), in the event of a severe stress on the financial system, you may have access to your bank accounts impaired or even frozen.

Even though the FDIC website states that "FDIC deposit insurance is backed by the full faith and credit of the United States government," there are no laws *requiring* the U.S. government to bail out the FDIC should events get out of hand.[12]

FDIC "insurance," in other words, is just another government promise. As of June 2011, the FDIC had only about $7.8 billion to insure about $9.7 trillion in assets—a shortfall of over 99 percent.[13] (See Figure 6.1.)

Of course, if the FDIC goes totally broke—as its chairman Sheila Bair intimated—it could tap its $500 billion credit line with the Treasury Department.[14] In that case the shortfall will only be 95 percent. In a fiscal emergency, what is the FDIC's promise going to be worth?

Why Your Financial Accounts May Not Be Safe: Bank "Holidays"

Famously, Franklin D. Roosevelt declared a "bank holiday" in March 1933, closing down banks and preventing account holders from accessing cash needed to run businesses or simply run households.[15]

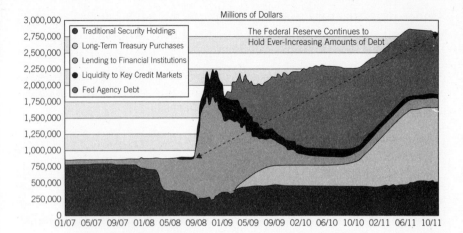

Figure 6.1   Toxic Assets Pile Up at the Fed

Source: Federal Reserve, cited in "8 Charts from a Brave New Banking and Economic System," My Budget 360 blog, December 29, 2011.

When the Herstatt Bank in Germany failed in 1974, several institutions were left holding the bag on unpaid obligations, as dollars that were supposed to be exchanged for deutsche mark payments got lost in the shuffle of liquidation.[16] In 2009, the U.S. government seized and closed 140 banks that it considered insolvent; in 2010, the number was over 157; in 2011, over 440[17] (see a trend here?).

In all of these cases, small depositors kept their money,[18] but even temporary closures can cause a business to grind to a halt or prevent a widow from paying for groceries. Although the MF Global brokerage is a futures trading firm and not a bank, its failure offers an instructive lesson in what might happen to your assets in the event of a bank holiday. There, the trustee elected to dump all customer assets, including gold, silver, cash, options, and commodities, into a single pool. Investors will be lucky if they eventually get back 70 percent of their account values.[19]

Ominously, one of the largest banks in the United States, Citigroup, began warning customers it may refuse to allow withdrawals. In April 2010, it began including this language in its account contracts:

> We reserve the right to require (7) days advance notice before permitting a withdrawal from all checking accounts.

Under pressure from worried customers, the bank later released a statement that it had been forced to enact the new policy as a result of Federal Reserve regulations, adding, "We have never exercised this right and have no plans to do so in the future."[20]

If you're a Citibank customer, best assume they mean "foreseeable future."

Save Your Pennies

In a further sign of dollar weakness, the White House asked Congress in its 2013 budget proposal for permission to debase the composition of our penny and nickel coins. *CNN Money* explains the move this way:

> The U.S. Mint is facing a problem . . . it costs more to make pennies and nickels than the coins are worth. . . . To be precise, it cost 2.4 cents to make one penny in 2011 and about 11.2 cents for each nickel.[21]

The switch, if it takes place, is bound to become yet another illustration of Gresham's law: Bad money drives out good.

Gresham's law was last seen operating in force in the United States in the mid-1960s, when pre-1965 dimes, quarters, and half-dollars—which contained 90 percent silver—were replaced with 75 percent copper substitutes.[22] Citizens began hoarding the silver-content coins (the "good" money) to avoid the loss of value associated with receiving the legally-mandated copper-content coins (the "bad" money). The hoarding promptly resulted in a shortage of coins in general circulation, until the Mint was able to churn out enough of the "bad" money to flood the market and drive out the "good."[23]

Why Gresham's Law Won't Be Repealed

"If you were one of those 1960s coin hoarders, those ordinary, pre-1965 dimes, quarters, and half-dollars are now worth $2.48, $6.20, and $12.41, respectively."

If you were one of those 1960s coin hoarders, those ordinary, pre-1965 dimes, quarters, and half-dollars are now worth $2.48, $6.20, and $12.41, respectively (February 2012 prices).[24]

Although today's pennies and nickels may not be worth the trouble of hoarding (you'll need warehouse-sized quantities if you hope to reap much future value), you may want to put a few rolls aside to show your grandchildren what real money used to look like . . .

Key Points

- Fixed-rate mortgages get cheaper as inflation drives down the value of your payment.
- Adjustable-rate loans dump the risk of inflation onto the consumer.
- Avoid foreclosure by renegotiating your loan with the bank or through legal delays and challenges.
- FDIC insurance may prove hollow in the event of a financial crisis.
- Access to your financial accounts may be legally restricted during fiscal emergencies or banking meltdowns.
- "Bad money drives out good": Look for the current penny and nickel to begin to disappear from circulation as our currency is debased.

CHAPTER

7

Dueling with the Devil:
Credit Cards and Student Loans

The biggest source of financial woe for most consumers is juggling credit card and student loan obligations. Credit card companies want to keep you indebted through easily manipulated contracts, and the new credit card law has only made things worse. Both credit cards and student loans may carry variable rates that will shoot up during periods of inflation. Options are limited, but there are ways of fighting back.

Why Credit Cards Aren't Worth the Plastic They're Printed On

You know what a contract is. Two parties enter into a binding agreement enforceable by law, for their mutual benefit. I run a farm and you run a restaurant. I agree to sell you eggs at so-much a dozen, and you agree to buy them.

You'd never enter a contract that the other party can change any time they want, whereas you have no rights to change anything, would you?

But do you know what's in your credit card contract? A few years back, Consumers Union took a stab at summarizing a typical contract in plain language. Updated to reflect changes in credit laws, I think today it might read something like this:

> Dear Credit Card Customer,
>
> Thank you for running up such an enormous balance. That low interest rate we promised you? We can raise it at any time, whenever whimsy strikes. If you don't like it, you can just take your business elsewhere.
>
> Want to transfer a card balance to us? Good. We'll charge you a balance transfer fee that you probably don't know about until it's too late because you didn't read the fine print. But we won't charge you any inactivity fees if you fail to use your card—that would be against the law. Instead we'll hit you with a big annual upfront fee for the privilege of even having a card.
>
> You have to get your payment to us 21 days from when we mail you the bill. Mail problems in either direction are now *your* problem. We'll cheerfully process your payment on the day we receive it—if we receive it before 9:01 A.M. Otherwise we'll process it the next day and charge you a late fee. Oh yeah, and our "bank" is open Sundays and holidays. Too bad if the post office didn't deliver your payment until Monday.
>
> If your payment is late even once, we'll charge you a $39 fee. Over limit? Expect an over limit fee. Cash advance? Cash advance fee. Spending money overseas? We'll take 3 percent of what you spend as well.
>
> So thanks, valuable chump, ah, strike that, I mean "customer." We look forward to servicing your account for a long, long time. . . .
>
> Sincerely,
>
> Your Credit Card Issuer[1]

Pretty one-sided, right? And all the credit card company has to do to change the interest rate you pay is send you a notice.

When superinflation hits, what do you think the credit card companies will do?

Don't Expect the New Law to Save You

While the recently passed Credit Card Act of 2009 has reigned in some of the worst credit card abuses (or at least made them more transparent), it's also introduced new tricks for card issuers to get your money.[2] The banks, after all, are desperate, because the Card Act is estimated to have killed almost $400 million a year in card fees.[3]

Interest rate hikes must now be preceded by 45 days' advance notice—unless you make a late payment, in which case all bets are off. If the bank changes the terms to something too odious for you to live with, you can opt out—turn in your card and take five years to pay off your balance under existing terms.

Of course, then you will have lost use of that card. But perhaps you will be eligible for a new "subprime credit card"—at a higher rate, of course.

Credit card companies used to be specific about what kind of infractions would trigger changes in interest rates, but increasingly they favor vague terms and conditions:

"New credit card terms are now almost like mysteries when it comes to figuring out what could cause your interest rates to increase and by how much," says Reed Allmand of Allmand Law. "The only way to combat this problem is to pay your balance every month and to pay it on time."[4]

Most credit card companies have now shortened the time-to-pay to the statutory 21 days, and have introduced tricks to cause late payments, like keeping open their banks on Sundays and holidays when your mail can't possibly be delivered.

How to Outwit the Credit Card Companies

Because credit card companies can change the terms of the "agreements" you sign with them by simply giving 45 days' notice, holding debt on credit cards when superinflation arrives is a formula for disaster. You can be sure that whatever the inflation rate shoots up to, your credit card rate will shoot up even higher.

The best way to outwit the credit card companies to opt out of their game. Opt out now, while rates are relatively low, pay down and pay off credit cards, and switch to debit cards instead. Debit cards have all the convenience of credit cards and none of the associated risk. Like credit cards, you can use them to keep track of your expenditures, buy things over the Internet and even rent cars.

(Of course, you can't use debit cards to overspend or make impulse purchases—but that's a good thing, right?)

How to Be a Bad Credit Card Customer

If you aren't in an immediate position to pay off your credit cards, create a plan to pay them down. Credit card companies will hate you because they want to keep you in debt. Here are a few strategies to pay off your cards faster.

- Pay more than the minimum payments. The minimum payments are calculated to keep you in maximum indebtedness for periods as long as 30 years. Do you still want to be paying for your toaster oven 30 years from now?
- Consolidate balances onto a low-interest-rate card. Make sure you know what you're getting into, though, because most low interest rates will disappear with a single late payment. Most banks now charge a balance transfer fee. Bankrate.com offers a calculator to make sure that it's actually cheaper to switch cards: http://www.bankrate.com/calculators/credit-cards/credit-card-balance-transfer-calculator.aspx
- Borrow against life insurance. Typically you'll be replacing a funny-money, the-rate-is-whatever-we-say payment with a fixed payment at fair rates. When superinflation hits, you want to be in fixed payments.
- Stop paying and use the leverage to renegotiate. Oddly enough, when credit card companies aren't getting regular payments, they become much more amenable to negotiating terms with you. After all, they are unsecured creditors. That means their prime legal recourse is to ding your credit report. (They might sue you as well, but in most states you'll get far better terms to pay off your judgment than you would paying 22 percent interest rates.)

Goose Your Contracts with a Gold Clause

If you are a small business owner, you are in the enviable position of protecting the value of your investments against future inflation by negotiating a gold clause payment.

A gold clause allows the creditor to collect payments in a specified amount of gold or gold equivalent. For instance, your contract might call for payment in 100 ounces of gold. If the value of gold in dollars goes up 10 times between now and the end of your contract, your creditor will have to pony up 10 times the dollars to pay you in the contracted amount of gold.

You will have effectively killed the risk of inflation.

Gold clauses were outlawed in the United States by the Gold Reserve Act of 1934, when FDR went looking for an excuse to end the gold standard.[5] But Congress reinstated their use in 1977 in accordance with 31 U.S.C. § 5118. In 2008, the U.S. Court of Appeal (Sixth Circuit) reaffirmed the use of the gold clause in *216 Jamaica Avenue, LLC vs. S&R Playhouse Realty LLC.* In that case, the Court held that a 1912 rental contract containing a gold clause was enforceable, raising the tenant's rent from $35,000 per year to $1.4 million per year.[6]

Further Reading on the Gold Clause

Before you write a gold clause into your next contract, learn more about the practice and its pitfalls from Henry Mark Holzer. Holzer is professor emeritus at Brooklyn Law School and he wrote the authoritative book on the subject: *The Gold Clause: What It Is and How to Use It Profitably* (San Jose: IUniverse.com, 2000).

How to Use Inflation to Discount Your Student Loans

Part 2's principle reminds us that future money is cheap money. If you can pay a fixed obligation you incur today (say, a $50,000 student loan) at some point in the future when the dollar is worth less, you are effectively getting a discount on your loan.

With student loan payments, that's easy if you qualify for a deferment. A deferment allows you to pay your federally subsidized loan back in the future without incurring any interest payment in the meantime. Here are a few ways you can qualify for a deferment:

- Go back to school.
- Get a medical internship or graduate fellowship.

- Become unemployed or financially unstable.
- Volunteer for the military or the Peace Corps.
- Have a child who requires parenting.
- Teach at a low-income school.[7]

Deferment conditions vary somewhat, depending on the type of loan a student carries (e.g., Stafford or Perkins loans). The Federal Student Aid site has created a handy chart summarizing the types of deferments available (see Table 7.1).

Don't confuse a deferment of your student loan with a forbearance. A forbearance allows you to begin paying your loan in the future, but accumulates interest, sometimes at an adjustable rate.[8]

Table 7.1   Student Loan Deferment Conditions

	Stafford Loans		Perkins Loans
Deferment Condition	Direct Loans[a,b]	FFEL Loans[a]	Perkins Loans
At least half-time study at a postsecondary school	YES	YES	YES
Study in an approved graduate fellowship program or in an approved rehabilitation training program for the disabled	YES	YES	YES
Unable to find full-time employment	Up to 3 years	Up to 3 years	Up to 3 years
Economic hardship (includes Peace Corps service)	Up to 3 years	Up to 3 years	Up to 3 years
Service listed under discharge/cancellation conditions	NO	NO	NO
Borrower is on active duty during a war or other military operation or national emergency and if the borrower was serving on or after Oct. 1, 2007, for an additional 180-day period following the demobilization date for the qualifying service	YES	YES	YES
For a borrower who is a member of the National Guard or other reserve component of the U.S. Armed Forces (current or retired) and is called or ordered to active duty while enrolled at least half-time at an eligible school or within six months of having been enrolled at least half-time, during the 13 months following the conclusion of the active duty service, or until the borrower returns to enrolled student status	YES	YES	YES

[a] For PLUS loans and unsubsidized Stafford loans only principal is deferred. Interest continues to accrue.
[b] Direct loan borrower who had an outstanding balance on an FFEL Loan first disbursed before July 1, 1993, when the borrower received his or her first direct loan, is eligible for additional deferments.

Source: StudentAid.ed.gov.

Check with your lender for details, but avoid a forbearance at all costs if you qualify for the more desirable deferment.

Beware of Prepaid Tuition Guarantees

If you're investing in a state 529 plan that purports to offer prepaid tuition at a state university at some time in the future—beware. The contract you think you are entering into may not be as ironclad as you think.

Nineteen states offer these popular investment accounts that "guarantee" future tuition for money paid in now, according to www .finaid.org, a student financial website. (Another 33 states offer college savings plans but without prepaid tuition guarantees.[9])

The prepaid plans purport to give parents peace of mind, "entitling" contract holders to receive future tuition and fee benefits, notwithstanding rises in college tuition prices (see Figure 7.1).[10] Plan managers invest the money in markets to grow the funds intended to pay the future costs.

But with tuition rates increasing at twice the general inflation rate and stock markets wobbling in an era of increased volatility, some 529 funds are in trouble.

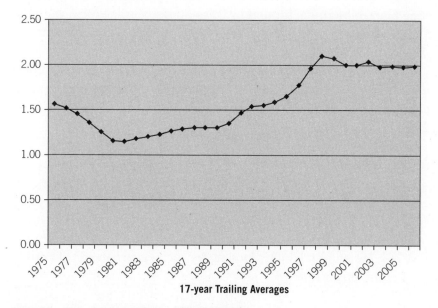

17-year Trailing Averages

Figure 7.1   Ratio of Tuition Inflation to General Inflation

Source: finaid.org.

Surprisingly to those relying on the 529 plans to lock in tuitions, only two of the 19 states (Florida and Texas) actually back their plan by the full faith and credit of the state.

Three others (Kentucky, Virginia, and West Virginia) have laws in place that set up special escrow accounts to meet shortfalls or require state institutions to accept less than full tuition if push comes to shove.

None of the other states offering prepaid tuition 529s actually require themselves to deliver the promised prepaid tuition, although three states (Illinois, Maryland, and South Carolina) do make legislatures "consider" a financial bailout for faltering plans.

529 Tuition Plans: Let the Buyer Beware

"None of [fourteen] states offering prepaid tuition 529s actually require themselves to deliver the promised prepaid tuition . . ."

In Illinois, a Crain's Chicago Business investigation revealed the state plan to be underfunded by 20 to 30 percent.[11] So far, the state legislature seems unwilling to ride to the rescue, putting parents on the hook for tuitions they thought they had already paid for.

A similar story is unfolding in Alabama, where Patti Lambert invested more than $100,000 in prepaid tuition for her eight grandchildren, only to learn that the plan may run out of money in 2015.

Said Ms. Lambert: "Everything about the way the plan was promoted implied that it was backed by the state."

How much are those implied guarantees worth? Consider this comment by Representative Jim Durkin of Alabama.

In a state beset by unbalanced budgets and unfunded pension obligations, "I guess the response would be, 'Get in line,'" he told the New York Times about families looking for their "guaranteed" tuitions.[12]

Let the buyer beware.

Key Points

- Contracts with credit card companies are subject to whimsical, one-sided changes for small infractions of rules—or no infractions at all.
- The Credit Card Act of 2009 eliminated some fees while instituting for banks a whole new way to play the game.
- Be a bad credit card customer: Pay down your balances quickly, or borrow against life insurance to change high-interest variable rates to a low fixed rate.
- Small businesses can once again write legally binding gold clauses into contracts.
- Use inflation to discount your student loans through a deferment loophole; don't confuse loan deferment with loan forbearance, where interest will continue to build up.
- States can default on prepaid tuition plans, even if you think you've locked in your child's tuition.

Diversify Out of Dollars

Minimize your exposure to dollars. Instead of having a huge savings account stuffed with dollars, keep a "basket" of investments that will rise in value in response to the government's inflation grab. That means real, tangible things like real estate, gold, and oil. It also means diversifying stocks and bonds (denominated in dollars) and getting paid in various non-dollar currencies. And it means managing your government-regulated accounts—IRAs, 401(k)s—to maximize inflation-hedging power.

CHAPTER

Fleeing the Dollar: Foreign Currencies

or years, investors fleeing financial instability have placed their bets on the U.S. dollar. But in a world awash with stimulus dollars, what foreign currencies are safe? All currencies are now fiat currencies—that is, money that derives its value from government law and regulation—and many are closely tied to the health of the U.S. dollar and the euro. Nonetheless, prudence dictates holding a portion of your wealth in a variety of non-dollar holdings.

The Dollar: From House of Bricks to House of Straw

Remember the story of the Three Little Pigs?

Pig #1 built a house of straw.
Pig #2 built a house of sticks.
Pig #3 built a house of bricks.

When a hungry Big Bad Wolf came by, he huffed and puffed and blew his way into the shabbily built houses of Pigs #1 and #2.
The pigs inside were delicious.
He couldn't blow down Pig #3's house, however, because it was so strong and sturdy.*

---

*He did break in through the chimney, however—but got roasted alive in a boiling pot. Moral: Quit when you're ahead.

The U.S. dollar used to be a house built of bricks, based on a growing economy, an enduring political system, budget surpluses, and low inflation. After World War II, the Bretton Woods Agreement ensured a stable foreign exchange system, with the dollar being convertible (between nations) to gold.[1]

The gold convertibility of Bretton Woods imposed a fiscal discipline on the federal government under which—during the Vietnam War—the nation increasingly chafed. The war created massive trade and balance-of-payments deficits, causing other nations to lose faith in the United States and demand gold for dollars. In 1971, President Nixon "closed the gold window," effectively cutting the dollar loose from the gold standard.[2] This *ipso facto* devaluation (in a preview of things to come) created massive inflation in the 1970s. Since then, federal budget surpluses have become immense deficits and the national debt has gone through the ceiling.[3] Oh, and the dollar has fallen 80 percent in value.[4]

The bricks had become sticks, but the dollar gradually stabilized at its new, lower value. With the Bretton Woods agreement shattered, the dollar accidentally became the world's reserve currency—that is, the most favored currency for global economic exchanges. The U.S. economy still dominated the world, the dollar was liquid, and there was, in fact, no currency alternative.[5]

But now the dollar's dominance is beginning to crack under the massive weight of federal deficits and ill-advised stimulus programs that have circulated trillions of new dollars. The dollar's perceived strength provided an excuse for policy makers to inflate and expand credit under a Keynesian economic model. Now exports are falling and investors are putting their money into other economies, notably China.[6]

In other words, the demand for U.S. dollars is falling at the exact moment the supply is massively increasing. Just as the U.S. dollar went from being a house of bricks to a house of sticks under the deficit spending of the Vietnam War, it is now on its way to going from a house of sticks to a house of straw under the nation's huge deficits.

It is only a matter of time before a strong wind—or a Big Bad Wolf—comes by to blow the dollar's house down.

The Dollar Near-Term: Temporary Upswing

As mismanaged as the dollar has been, it still benefits from the United States' reputation for stability. Increasingly, that reputation will be tested in the coming years and found to be an illusion. Until then, however, the dollar's wooden house seems a lot sturdier than the straw houses of other countries.

In particular, investors fleeing the weakened euro will create a short-term rush to the perceived safety of the U.S. dollar, shoring up its value in 2012. CNBC news anchor Brian Sullivan predicts that the eurozone bailout will cost the European central banks some $2 trillion and that the euro will reach parity with the dollar by the end of 2012.[7] And relative to other world economies, the United States has been showing weak signs of growth—a 3 percent GDP growth in the last quarter of 2011 and a modest drop in unemployment.[8]

But in the long run, the dollar is in trouble. Long-term U.S. interest rates are already rising as the market begins to perceive the inflation threat of rising global oil and commodity prices and the huge expansion of money supply.[9] China has been making steady progress toward internationalizing the yuan, with Chinese banks in Hong Kong increasingly settling transactions in that currency. As the world gradually shuns the dollar as the currency of international exchange, the dollar will begin to fall.

Dr. Barry Eichengreen, a professor of economics and political science at the University of California, Berkeley, estimates that the loss of reserve currency status will cause the dollar to fall by 20 percent. "Because the prices of imported goods will rise in the U.S., living standards will be reduced by about 1.5 percent of GDP . . . Americans will definitely feel it in the wallet."[10]

A 2008 report to Congress by the Congressional Research Service warns, however, that the transition may not be smooth.

> The critical factor governing whether orderly and disorderly adjustment of international imbalances occurs is foreign investor expectations about future dollar depreciation. Rational expectations will have a smoothing effect on the size

of international capital flows. In contrast, a sharp plunge of the dollar is likely to occur if investors do not form rational expectations. If the dollar then depreciates at a rate faster than foreign investors now expect, a dollar crisis becomes likely. Currently foreign investors do not appear to have a realistic expectation of future dollar depreciation. A dollar crisis could start when they realize their error and try to move quickly out of dollar assets—the likely stampede would cause a "dollar crisis."[11]

If anything, financial prospects for the dollar have worsened since this report to Congress.

Foreign Currencies: Risks and Rewards

Diversifying out of the U.S. dollar and into foreign currencies might seem a no-brainer investment to provide safe harbor as dollar inflation asserts itself. However, when you buy a foreign currency, you are also assuming the political and other risks of investing in that foreign country—which may or may not manage its economy better than the United States does.

Foreign Currencies: Keep Your Eyes Open

"When you buy a foreign currency, you are also assuming the political and other risks of investing in that foreign country—which may or may not manage its economy better than the United States does."

Foreign investor expectations also come into play when determining the value of the dollar. Although the American economy is becoming a shambles, many foreign investors fear that their local economy is becoming a worse shambles, and faster. Investing in America in times of uncertainty, they drive up the value of the dollar vis-à-vis other currencies. And the world is currently full of uncertainties: atomic weapons in Iran, war in Afghanistan, changing regimes across the Middle East, terrorist attacks in India and the United States, and a European international debt crisis.

The bottom line: Foreign currency shifts are very hard to predict, so investing in foreign currencies takes on an aspect of speculating more than long-term investing. The bottom may indeed drop out of the dollar—but it could drag other major currencies to the bottom with it.

Which Currencies Should I Invest In?

Even knowing that investing in foreign currencies can be a risky business, there are still reasons you may want to invest a portion of your money in non-dollar currencies. Perhaps you have a home or do business in foreign countries, or maybe you fear seizure of your gold or property assets in the event of a dollar collapse.

During the 1970s Great Inflation in the United States, the dependable Swiss franc performed quite well. But the Swiss franc isn't what it used to be. In the 1970s, the franc was a hard money currency backed 40 percent by gold, but in 1999 the Swiss government abandoned that commitment when it joined the International Monetary Fund.[12]

As the dollar and the Swiss franc went, so went the rest of the world. Currently, there are no currencies anywhere in the world that are not "managed" in one form or another by their issuing governments.

All currencies are now fiat currencies, from the Japanese yen to the euro. As the oddsmaker says, "You pays yer money and you takes yer choice."

The Chinese Yuan Is Going Up—for Now

For years China has kept the Chinese yuan (also known as the renminbi, or RMB) artificially undervalued against the U.S. dollar, initially through a fixed peg that began in 1994, and starting in 2005 through a peg to a basket of currencies that allowed it to rise over 25 percent by 2011.[13, 14]

At the 2011 G20 summit in Cannes, however, China reached an agreement with the West to move "more rapidly toward a more market-determined exchange rate system." Said British Prime Minister David Cameron: "China has determined to increase exchange rate flexibility."

(To save face, China's name was deleted from the draft of the final document. Washington also promised "to adopt policies to build confidence and support growth and implement clear, credible, and specific measures" to improve the economy. Good luck with that.)[15]

Meanwhile, in Congress, there is pressure from both Democrats and Republicans to force China to revalue its currency. This will address imbalances in wages, environmental controls, and intellectual property theft that give China an unfair advantage.[16]

If Washington has its way, however, the dollar will be devalued against the yuan, reducing imports and increasing inflationary pressure in the United States as all those cheap Chinese goods suddenly become more expensive to Americans.

The process is already under way: In the last half of 2011, the yuan appreciated nearly 12 percent against the dollar on an inflation-adjusted basis.[17] One scholar, Joshua Lipman of the University of Pennsylvania's Wharton School, recently undertook an analysis of the yuan's purchasing power and found it undervalued by 37.5 percent.[18]

Over the next few years, expect China to gradually open foreign trading channels with the yuan as the country continues to shake its ties to the ailing U.S. dollar.

Although the Chinese government imposes tight restrictions on currency exchanges, there are several ways available for Americans to invest in the yuan.

You can exchange dollars directly by opening a Bank of China RMB personal or business savings account. The account has strict limits on how much can be exchanged or remitted: $4,000 worth of renminbi a day, up to a maximum of $20,000 a year. Because the accounts are non-interest-bearing, account holders are betting on a continued rise in the RMB vis-à-vis the dollar.[19] And you cannot deposit or withdraw cash in RMB, only in dollars, which will incur a small conversion fee.[20]

Market Vectors Chinese Renminbi/USD ETN (symbol: CNY) uses derivatives like three-month currency forward contracts to index the yuan. WisdomTree Dreyfus also has a Chinese yuan exchange-traded fund (symbol: CYB). Since both the CNY and CYB funds are based on currency forward contracts, over the short term they can and do diverge from the actual price of the yuan based on market expectations of future yuan prices.

In June 2011, Guinness Atkinson Funds launched the Renminbi Yuan & Bond Fund, a mutual fund that invests largely in yuan-denominated bonds (symbol: GARBX) of multinational and Chinese corporations. It also holds a substantial percent of its assets in cash, possibly because the fund has not yet had time to find suitable investments.

Finally, a gold bullion exchange in Hong Kong, the Chinese Gold & Silver Exchange Society (CGSE), began in October trading gold contracts denominated in Chinese yuan.[21] The Renminbi Kilobar Gold contracts are being promoted as "double safe havens" because investors' money is in both yuan and gold (but of course some investors see "double safe havens" as double exposure to gold and yuan risks). The contracts are traded electronically during local business hours (with provisions for suspending trading during heavy typhoons.) A HK$3 per contract (per side) fee is levied on all transactions. The contracts are regulated by the Chinese government, which for now limits foreign purchases to no more than 20 billion yuan per year.[22] More information the CGSE contracts may be found at http://www.cgse.com.hk/en/product_08.php.

Beware: China Has Its Own Stimulus Problems

While exchanging dollars for yuan may seem like a slam-dunk, proceed with caution.

China reacted to the Great Recession (which caused a 43 percent hit on Chinese exports) with its own stimulus program, opening the credit spigots and unleashing an estimated 18 trillion yuan in new financing in just two years. According to Jonathan Lee, senior director of financial institutions of Fitch Ratings, "This is the equivalent of 55 percent of China's GDP."[23] Much of this new debt went into financing infrastructure investments and local governments.

With that magnitude of loans floating around, Fitch downgraded its outlook on China's long-term local currency debt to negative on expectations that some portion of those loans will not perform.

What percentage? Chinese officials peg the number at 2 percent, but Credit Suisse Group AG analysts peg it at 8 to 12 percent. Chinese banks will be hard hit because as much as 40 to 60 percent of their equity may be held in real estate and local government loans likely to go bad. Credit Suisse singled out the Agricultural Bank of China Ltd. and Chongquing Rural Commercial Bank as two institutions likely to "underperform."[24]

Another danger of China's stimulus binge: inflation. The flood of new money in China has goosed values of everything from real estate to food. China's official inflation rate of 5.5 percent undoubtedly understates the real inflation rate by a large amount.[25]

Conclusion: China's renminbi will rise as the Chinese economy continues its growth curve, but some of the same inflationary forces at work on the dollar are also at work on the yuan.

The Euro: Slow-Motion Meltdown

The euro was created in 1999 as the European alternative to the dollar. Eleven nations—Austria, Belgium, Finland, France, Germany, Ireland, Italy, Luxembourg, the Netherlands, Portugal, and Spain—agreed to replace their national currencies with the single euro, creating an economic bloc that would rival the hegemony of the U.S. dollar in international trade.[26] The hope was that wide acceptance of the euro would lend to it a "reserve currency" status, sparking a competitive advantage for European debt offerings and trade.[27]

The euro has been a huge success at breaking down trade barriers between the peoples of Europe. The original 11 member nations have been joined by 16 others, from Estonia to Malta, and today over 330 million people use the common currency—20 percent of the world's economic activity.[28, 29] (See Figure 8.1.) To join the euro, countries have to meet strict economic guidelines: a budget deficit of less than 3 percent of GDP, national debt less than 60 percent of GDP, low inflation, and interest rates on parity with the rest of the European Union.[30]

However, the implementation of the euro had a fatal flaw: Once a nation was in the club, there was no effective way to control

Figure 8.1   The 27 Member States of the European Union

Source: eucountrylist.com.

irresponsible economic behavior by its free-spending members. Trade imbalances developed, with thrifty, high-productivity countries like Germany benefiting, while stagnating economies like Portugal, Italy, and Greece suffered.[31]

The problems reached a flash point in Greece, where years of deficit spending pushed the national debt to some 1½ times of GDP.[32] Investors—fearing their money was at risk—began pushing up rates for Greek bonds to unprecedented levels (20 percent on a three-year bond), making it impossible for Greece to refinance its debts.[33, 34]

The crisis soon evolved to encompass other high-risk euro economies, among them Ireland, Portugal, and Italy. All ran huge deficits, and had national debts of over 95 percent of GDP.[35] Rather than expelling bankrupt members—which would have at least allowed the errant countries to devalue their national currencies to regain balance with reality—European leaders began offering a series of bailouts, first to defend Greek bonds, then gradually extending the eurozone bailout fund to Ireland, Portugal, and finally Italy.[36]

Italy's debt problem, however, dwarfs that of smaller troubled euro countries by an order of magnitude. Its $2.4 trillion public debt is five times larger than that of Greece, 11 times larger than Portugal's, and 12 times that of Ireland.[37]

Italy is, literally, too big to fail, and if it does it will take the euro down with it. In December 2011, Standard & Poor's rating agency placed 15 European nations on its negative Creditwatch, "prompted by [its] belief that stresses in the eurozone have risen in recent weeks to the extent that they now put downward pressure on the credit standing of the eurozone as a whole." The factors it cites:

- Tightening credit conditions across the eurozone.
- Markedly higher risk premiums on a growing number of eurozone sovereigns, including some that are currently rated AAA.
- Continuing disagreements among European policy makers on how to tackle the immediate market confidence crisis and, longer term, how to ensure greater economic, financial, and fiscal convergence among eurozone members.
- High levels of government and household indebtedness across a large area of the eurozone.
- The rising risk of economic recession in the eurozone as a whole in 2012. Currently, [it] expects output to decline next year in countries such as Spain, Portugal, and Greece, but [it] now assigns a 40 percent probability of a fall in output for the eurozone as a whole.[38]

The euro, in other words, is a basket case. Investors are already being required to take a 50 percent haircut on Greek bond repayments, and austerity measures in Greece and Italy (along with forced changes in political leadership) are likely to prove to be too little, too late.[39] Financial decisions undertaken in Europe have to be approved by all 17 leaders of the eurozone, and then have to be sold by those leaders to all 17 countries.[40] This ungainly and bureaucratic process itself contributes to the crises, preventing effective and early action.

Comments Keynesian economist Paul Krugman:

> Never mind Greece, whose economy is to Europe roughly as greater Miami is to the United States. At this point, markets have lost faith in the euro as a whole, driving up interest rates even for countries like Austria and Finland, hardly known for profligacy. And it's not hard to see why. The combination of austerity-for-all and a central bank morbidly obsessed with inflation makes it essentially impossible for indebted countries to escape from their debt trap and is, therefore, a recipe for widespread debt defaults, bank runs, and general financial collapse.[41]

Krugman, of course, wants to open the sluice gates of the eurozone bailout fund even wider, but the demands of the failed euro states would prove a bottomless pit.

In the end, a breakup of the currency union seems inevitable. In a best-case scenario, there will be an orderly exit of countries like Greece and Italy from the union, leaving a fiscally sound, smaller core. A worse-case scenario would see investors' confidence in the euro plummet, leading to mounting interest rates, sovereign defaults, and last-minute attempts by the European Central Bank and the U.S. Federal Reserve to shore up the euro before its final collapse.

An abrupt collapse would be catastrophic, both for the people of Europe and for the United States. While European investors seeking safety will temporarily pump up the American dollar, American banks and hedge and market funds hold at least a trillion dollars in European risk, and provided $518 billion in loan guarantees to Greece, Italy, Ireland, Portugal, and Spain in the first half of 2011.[42] In other words, at the precise moment the European economy is in a shambles, the American economy will begin to unravel as well. Lending will cease, companies will shed jobs, and consumer confidence will be shot. Result: a deep worldwide recession and more inflationary pressure on the dollar as the Fed prints even more money to lubricate the gear of commerce.

If you're not invested in the euro, don't. And if you are, get out.

One Way to Invest in Foreign Currencies: ETFs

Regardless of what currency you are interested in, the easiest way to invest in foreign currencies is by purchasing exchange-traded funds (ETFs) that hold foreign currency assets. You will be buying direct exposure to the currency you wish to hold (along with the previously discussed risks of all ETFs, i.e., exposure to credit risk and dangers of system failure in the event of a fiscal meltdown.)

There are dozens of foreign currency ETFs. Table 8.1 shows a list of the most commonly traded currencies and their stock exchange symbols.

How to Invest in Foreign Bonds

Another way for U.S. investors to invest in foreign currencies is to invest indirectly by buying foreign bonds or a foreign bond mutual fund directly through your brokerage account.

Table 8.1   Foreign Currency Exchange-Traded Funds

Currency	Symbol
Australian dollar	FXA
Brazilian real	BZF
British pound	FXB
Canadian dollar	FXC
Chinese yuan	CYB
Euro	FXE
Indian rupee	ICN
Japanese yen	FXY
Mexican peso	FXM
New Zealand dollar	BNZ
Russian ruble	XRU
Swedish krona	FXS
Swiss franc	FXF

Source: *Seekingalpha.com*, A Guide to Currency ETFs and ETNS; *Stocks-simplified.com*, Best Foreign Currency ETF List.

Because the bond is denominated in foreign currency, its value will rise against the dollar as the dollar declines. For example, purchasers of Canadian government bonds in 2009 benefited from the price appreciation of the Canadian dollar, which was trading at $.81 per dollar at the beginning of the year but about $.95 at the end of the year, a 15 percent increase.[43]

Another way to indirectly own foreign currency is to invest in an international bond fund, which owns baskets of bonds from a number of non-U.S. countries. Table 8.2 shows a list of top performers, with five-year annualized returns of over 8 percent and small exposure to the U.S. dollar.[44]

Another way to purchase a basket of currencies is to buy into products that invest primarily in debt issued by governments other than the United States.

SPDR Barclays International Treasury Bond ETF (symbol: BWX) and S&P/Citigroup International Treasury Fund (symbol: IGOV) buy treasury bonds issued by developed countries (e.g., Japan, Germany, France, Italy) with an average maturity of 6.5 to 8.4 years.

Table 8.2   Top-Performing International Bond Funds

Fund Name	Symbol	Ann. Ret.
Templeton Global Bond Adv	TGBAX	12.52%
Templeton Global Bond A	TPINX	12.25%
Templeton Global Bond R	FGBRX	11.98%
Templeton Global Bond C	TEGBX	11.79%
Maxim Global Bond	MXGBX	11.58%
Oppenheimer International Bond Y	OIBYX	9.06%
PIMCO Foreign Bond (Unhedged) I	PFUIX	8.81%
PIMCO Foreign Bond (Unhedged) P	PFUPX	8.70%
Oppenheimer International Bond A	OIBAX	8.66%
PIMCO Foreign Bond (Unhedged) Adm	PFUUX	8.49%

Source: MSN Money, Yahoo! Finance.

For shorter-term maturities (1 to 3 years), investigate SPDR Barclays Capital Short-Term International Treasury Bond ETF (symbol: BWZ) and S&P/Citigroup's 1–3 Year International Treasury Fund (symbol: ISHG)

Note: Check the asset allocation of the bond fund you are considering purchasing to be sure it is investing in countries you consider a prudent risk. Some of these funds may be heavily invested in countries like Italy or Spain, or hold a large percentage of assets in U.S. Treasuries.

Low-Debt Countries = Good Bond Bets

Investors, rightly, have been fleeing the bonds of the PIGS—Portugal, Italy, Greece, and Spain. These countries face massive deficits dragging their economy underwater. Greece and Italy are the worst offenders, with debts of 159 percent and 119 percent of their gross national product, respectively.[45] (See Table 8.3.)

The market price of credit default swaps gives an estimate of investor sentiment as to the probability of defaulting. By this measure, Greece has a 98 percent chance of blowing off its debt repayment in the next five years.[46] Other countries most likely to default? Venezuela, Argentina, Pakistan, and Ukraine, according to the ratings from Credit Market Analysis, which markets pricing data to hedge firms.[47]

But why buy bonds from PIGS when you can make the opposite play—buying bonds of low-debt nations like Norway, Australia, South Korea, and New Zealand. Chance of default in these well-managed, industrialized countries is slim (4 percent, for instance, in the case of Norway).[48]

According to William Larkin, portfolio manager for Cabot Money Management, "The best method to gain access to these specific markets is either through exchange-traded funds, mutual funds, or closed-end mutual funds."

Playing ETFs is easy for Australia and New Zealand:

- Australia: Australian Dollar Trust (symbol: FXA)
- New Zealand: WisdomTree Dreyfus New Zealand Dollar ETF (symbol: BNZ)

Table 8.3   Europe's Debtor Nations

Country	Currency Unit	% of GDP (3Q '11)
Greece	euro	159.1
Italy	euro	119.6
Portugal	euro	110.1
Ireland	euro	104.9
Belgium	euro	98.5
France	euro	85.2
United Kingdom	GBP	85.2
Hungary	HUF	82.6
Germany	euro	81.8
Austria	euro	71.6
Malta	euro	70.3
Cyprus	euro	67.5
Spain	euro	66.0
Netherlands	euro	64.5
Poland	PLN	56.3
Denmark	DKK	49.3
Finland	euro	47.2
Latvia	LVL	44.6
Slovenia	euro	44.4
Slovakia	euro	42.2
Czech Republic	CZK	39.8
Lithuania	LTL	37.6
Sweden	SEK	37.0
Romania	RON	33.3
Luxembourg	euro	18.5
Bulgaria	BGN	15.0
Estonia	euro	6.1

Source: Eurostat, *Euro Area Government Debt down to 87.4% of GDP.*
Euroindicators, Eurostat, February 6, 2012, http://epp.eurostat.ec.europa.eu/
cache/ITY_PUBLIC/2-06022012-AP/EN/2-06022012-AP-EN.PDF.

There are no ETFs currently linked to either the Norwegian krone or the South Korean won. Investors with $100,000 or more to spend can buy bonds in these countries directly from their brokers.

Others may want to invest in stocks of these countries on the theory that their favorable governmental balance sheets will spill over to private equity markets.

For Norway, one option is the Global X FTSE Nordic 30 ETF (symbol: GTF). This is a single-country ETF that seeks to capture the broad equity performance of Norway, with about 20 percent weight in financials.[49]

For South Korea, the iShares MSCI South Korea Index Fund (symbol: EWY) invests in a diversified spectrum of roughly 100 actively traded South Korean stocks, including global corporations like Samsung Electronics and Hyundai Motor Co.[50]

Gold Private Currency

The uneasiness many people feel with fiat (nonbacked) paper currency has led several entrepreneurial companies to offer what is, in essence, private currency denominated in gold.

GoldMoney is the biggest and arguably the most reputable of these companies, holding over 600,000 ounces of gold and 25 million ounces of silver on deposit as backing for its "goldgrams" unit of currency.[51] GoldMoney is assessable and approved for IRAs, and can be used to directly pay other members of the GoldMoney network, or sold and converted back into U.S. dollars or various foreign currencies like Japanese yen and Canadian dollars.

GoldMoney customers have 100 percent allocated ownership of their metals and can take physical delivery at any time. Transactions made with goldgrams are subject to a one percent fee up to a very small maximum. For instance, a goldgram payment of $50 costs $0.50 in transaction fees, whereas a payment of $50,000 costs $5.13.[52]

Another company offering digital gold currencies is Pecunix, founded in 2002. As of July 2011, they had some 2.7 million ounces of gold in storage for their account holders.[53]

Because companies offering digital gold currency are private and unregulated, users are subject to dangers of fraud and mismanagement. Several digital gold companies have gone out of business, and in 2007 the U.S Department of Justice indicted the owners of e-gold on money-laundering charges.[54] (Depositors' assets were frozen and liquidated returns are, four years later, being made available under a court agreement.)[55]

Avoiding Digital Gold Fraud

The Global Digital Currency Association, an industry group, maintains a Fraud List of companies and websites it deems shady at: http://www.gdcaonline .org/?target=frauds

---

Both GoldMoney and Pecunix offer a bullion audit trail. While these are the best established companies, there are other players in the digital gold market (see Table 8.4). (Again, this is an unregulated marketplace. Investigate carefully before committing your assets.)

Become a Foreign Farmer

You can simultaneously invest in a tangible asset and diversify out of U.S. dollars by investing in farmland in foreign countries like Canada, Argentina, or even Bulgaria.

Table 8.4   Private Money Companies

Company	Website
BullionVault	bullionvault.com
C-gold	c-gold.com
e-dinar	e-dinar.com
EuroGoldCash	eurogoldcash.com
gbullion	gbullion.com
GoldMoney	goldmoney.com
iGolder	igolder.com
LibertyReserve	libertyreserve.com
Pecunix	pecunix.com

Source: Digital Gold Currency magazine, November 2011.

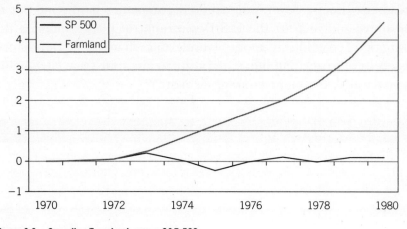

Figure 8.2   Canadian Farmland versus S&P 500
Note: Chart Rebased on 1970 to "0."
Source: AgCapita Newsletter, Vol. 1, No. 13, July 18, 2008.

World population just passed the 7 billion mark and biofuels are diverting crops from food use, increasing demand for fertile farmland all over the world. Long-term drought has already cut wheat and rice yields in Australia by one-third and may be a harbinger of global climate change.[56]

Canadian farmland investment fund AgCapita points out that in the early 1970s period of high inflation, Canadian farmland investment yielded roughly 16 percent a year, compared to the S&P 500 index yield of 2 percent. (See Figure 8.2.)

Canada is a politically stable country with a huge agricultural infrastructure. AgCapita Farmland Investment Partnership LP is closed, but a second fund, AgCapita Farmland Fund II LP offers limited partnership investment vehicles with a $5,000 minimum investment. AgCapita focuses on farmland in Western Canada, primarily in the province of Saskatchewan.

Many Latin American countries also have fertile farmlands, particularly Argentina, with its diverse climate and highly developed agricultural sector. There are few easy investment vehicles for buying farmland in this part of the world. One, however, is the DGC Asset Management's Greenfield Development, which has put under cultivation 15,000 hectares of previously unused land in

Latin America. The minimum investment is £10,000. For a larger minimum investment (£20,000), investors can also participate in DGC syndicates that directly invest in farmland leasebacks in the United Kingdom. Non–U.S. citizens may want to take a look at GreenWorld BVI, which offers direct investments in farmland in Africa, Australia, and Europe.

The risks of owning foreign farmland are the same as the risks outlined in Chapter 3 for U.S. farmland ("Risks of Farmland Investing"), with the additional risk burden of political corruption or instability.

Key Points

- The dollar used to be a house of bricks; now it's become a house of straw.
- Nonetheless, in the short term the dollar will benefit from investors fleeing even weaker currencies.
- By design, the Chinese yuan is going up—for now. But China has its own problems.
- The euro will continue its slow-motion meltdown as problems with the PIGS (Portugal, Italy, Greece, and Spain) drag it down.
- Bonds of low-debt nations like Norway, Australia, South Korea, and New Zealand are a good bet.
- Private, gold-denominated currencies are worth a look.
- Farmland investments in stable countries like Canada and Australia provide both a tangible asset and currency diversification.

CHAPTER

Manage Your Government-Regulated Accounts

Most IRAs offer few choices to hedge against the coming wave of inflation—yet penalize owners who want to move money elsewhere. In some plans it may be possible to invest in commodity funds, indexes, or TIPS that will provide some moderate protection—though each has its dangers. With rising taxes a surety, it may also make sense to convert your traditional IRA to a Roth plan. Finally, more aggressive investors will want to start a self-directed IRA, which will enable them to take advantage of many other inflation-hedging strategies.

The Threat to Your IRA Wealth

For most Americans, a sizable portion of their wealth is tied up in an IRA, usually invested in mutual funds tightly tied to the value of the dollar. That's great as long as the dollar is strong and stable, but in times of inflation, dollar-denominated stocks and stock funds will fall in purchasing price along with the dollar.

Bonds and bond funds are no solution. Short-term bonds such as T-bills are low risk, but with commensurate low returns (less than 0.25 percent per year.) Long-term bond rates are also low (less than 3.25 percent per year) and embody current inflationary expectations.[1] But if inflation is higher than anticipated, interest rates will go up. Bond prices are therefore vulnerable to being hammered down by dollar weakness, resulting in a double loss of value for the holders—once on the spread between bond rate and inflation rate, and once on price weakness caused by inflation.

Two Mutual Funds You Can Buy to Hedge against Inflation

Commodity-linked funds provide a way to invest in commodity contracts that track commodity prices closely. In accordance with the principle to "invest in real things," you can move part of your IRA money out of stock and bond funds into one of two commodity-linked funds available to most investors.

The first, the Oppenheimer Real Asset A fund (symbol: QRAAX), tracks the Goldman Sachs Commodity Index and invests in "a broad range of commodity sectors, including energy, precious metals, industrial metals, agriculture, and livestock." It is heavily weighted (almost 70 percent) to the energy sector.[2]

PIMCO Commodity Real Return Strategy fund (symbol: PCRIX) tracks the Dow Jones-AIG Commodity Total Return Index, which is more of a broad-based market basket of assorted commodities and therefore less susceptible to energy price movements.

Both the PIMCO and Oppenheimer products trade in futures contracts, creating some credit risk exposure. And because commodity prices can rise and fall quickly, if you trade in these funds, expect sharp swings in price movement.

U.S. Treasury Bonds: "Certificates of Guaranteed Confiscation"

Assuming your objective is to obtain a reasonable return on your investment capital, there is little to recommend in owning U.S. Treasury bonds. The purchasing power of the U.S. dollar has sunk 64 percent in the last 30 years.[3] Assume for a moment that Treasury bonds do just as "well" for the next three decades. Not even allowing for the growth of your capital, 30-year U.S. Treasury notes need to yield 4 percent just for the government to return your money to you unharmed.

Before his inauguration, then president-elect Obama made this candid prediction:

> We're already looking at a trillion-dollar budget deficit or close to a trillion-dollar budget deficit, and . . . potentially we've got trillion-dollar deficits for years to come . . .[4]

Take the president at his word. The dollar is being debased at an ever-increasing rate. The Fed is holding short-term interest rates at an artificial low that must soon end, and long-term rates are rising in anticipation of a spike in inflation.

With their current spending binge, Congress has put into place spending and entitlement programs that will require unprecedented amounts of borrowing for decades. Do you think the U.S. dollar will be as sound over the next three decades as over the last three?[5]

Certificates of Guaranteed Confiscation

Far from being the safe, foolproof investment of years past, U.S. Treasury bonds are developing into sure-fire wealth deflators—or, as economist Dr. Franz Pick calls them, "certificates of guaranteed confiscation."

Twisting in the Wind

In September of 2011, after two failed rounds of "quantitative easing," the Federal Reserve unveiled its latest effort to spur the economy—Operation Twist. Operation Twist is a $400 billion plan to drive down interest rates on 10-year Treasury bonds. The Fed is selling some of its trillion dollars in medium-term bonds to purchase longer-term bonds like the 10-year Treasuries, to which many other rates—including mortgage rates—are tied.[6]

However, the effort to revive the housing market has had little effect. Mortgage rates at the start of the program were already near record lows, and even lower rates will only serve to make homes more affordable for those with stellar credit to whom cautious banks will actually agree to lend.[7] Operation Twist did seem to give a short, one-month bounce to the stock market and arguably was in part responsible for a 0.4 percent decrease in the U.S. unemployment rate in November 2011.[8, 9]

All in all, Operation Twist has had little effect on the housing or employment market and simply has served to discourage investors from buying bonds. It is not a substitute for addressing structural problems with the American economy and may even serve to widen income inequality. Comments Daniel Indiviglio of the *Atlantic*:

> The Fed's action will leave those in the worst situations hoping for a mere trickle-down effect. A handful might find jobs a little sooner, but the rest will be left either renting or living in a home with a relatively high mortgage interest rate. And many of those borrowers will remain underwater. . . . Those who are unable to benefit from the low interest rates will have the same after-housing disposable incomes as before.[10]

TIPS: Inflation Protection or Inflation Fraud?

As fears about inflation have justly grown, the U.S. Treasury has offered Treasury inflation-protected securities (TIPS). These are bonds that guarantee you a fixed rate of return whatever the underlying inflation rate turns out to be. The coupon rate remains constant through the 5-, 10-, 20-, or 30-year life of the bond, but the principal is constantly adjusted according to a multiplier based on the Consumer Price Index (CPI).[11]

Investors can buy TIPS directly from the U.S. Treasury (http://www.treasurydirect.gov/) or invest in any one of a number of inflation-protected securities funds. Here are a few of the largest:

- ING BlackRock Inflation-Protected Bond Fund (symbol: IBRIX)
- Transamerica PIMCO Real Return TIPS Fund (symbol: IRRAX)
- Principal Inflation Protection Fund (symbol: PITAX)
- John Hancock II Real Return Bond Fund (symbol: JIRRX)
- MFS Inflation-Adjusted Bond Fund (symbol: MIAAX)
- American Century Inflation-Protected Bond Fund (symbol: APOAX)
- Franklin Real Return Fund (symbol: FRRAX)

Theoretically, investing in TIPS or an inflation-protected fund should protect holders from the pain of inflation, but because the government issues the CPI on which it is based, in practice results may vary.

Why You Can't Trust Government Inflation Statistics

The CPI is supposed to measure "the cost of maintaining a constant standard of living," but it purposely excludes some cost areas that are rising rapidly, such as energy costs and income taxes.[12] Further, periodically the "market basket" of goods and services is adjusted to take into account changes in living habits, bringing an air of subjectivity to the basis of the numbers.[13] Because many budget items like Social Security payments are directly linked to changes in the CPI, it is in the government's interest to understate the rate of inflation. Says J. Roger Shealy of SKadvisors, "If you can't win the game, change the rules."[14]

When CPI figures are calculated using the same methodology in effect just eight years ago, the inflation rate is consistently 3 to 4 percent higher than the currently reported CPI, as Figure 9.1 shows.

Thus, investors in TIPS may believe they are protecting their money against inflation, but will still be losing 4 percent purchasing power each year. John Williams of American Business Analytics & Research runs an instructive website, ShadowStats.com, that more fully describes government hanky-panky with the CPI and other government data.

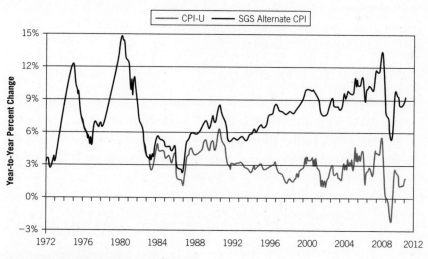

Figure 9.1   Old CPI versus New, 1972–2011

Source: ShadowStats.com, BLS.

Losing Ground with TIPS

"Investors in TIPS may believe they are protecting their money against inflation, but will still be losing 4 percent purchasing power each year."

Finally, how many TIPS investors are aware that the Department of the Treasury reserves the right to substitute another index of its choosing for the CPI index?

> If, while an inflation-indexed security is outstanding, the CPI is (1) discontinued, (2) in the judgment of the Secretary, fundamentally altered in a manner materially adverse to the interests of an investor in the security, or (3) in the judgment of the Secretary, altered by legislation or Executive Order in a manner materially adverse to the interests of an investor in the security, Treasury, after consulting with the BLS, *will substitute an appropriate alternative index.*[15]

Italics added. Imagine what this will mean in an era of hyperinflation.

In plain English: At the very moment when investors most need to be protected—i.e., when the CPI is going through the roof—the Treasury Department can stop indexing TIPS to the CPI and arbitrarily substitute a different index.

What to Hold in Your IRA

Many company IRAs offer limited investment menus in their IRA plans, making inflation-hedging choices difficult. On the most basic level, stock index funds offer one way to outrun a loss of purchasing power, at least during times of mild inflation. Index funds are stock funds that simply own all of the stocks that they are tracking. Not only do index funds often outperform managed funds, but fees and commissions are much lower. Vanguard, for instance, offers funds that track the S&P 500, short-term government bonds, and many international indexes.

Some IRAs will permit investing in various "inflation-protected" funds, such as the PIMCO, American Century, or John Hancock funds listed under the discussion of TIPS. Despite their shortfalls, a TIPS fund might be better than nothing at hedging your assets if it is the only alternative for your IRA.

Alternatively, some companies offer a "self-directed 401(k)" option that provides some of the benefits of a self-directed IRA. A self-directed 401(k) option isn't as flexible as an actual self-directed IRA (see below), but it is a good half measure if you are tied to a company IRA.[16] Under a self-directed 401(k), you can, for instance, directly invest in energy, timber, or mining stocks discussed elsewhere in this book, or trade in ETFs like the ones listed for gold, silver, and oil.

Start a Self-Directed IRA

If your employer's IRA plan has limited investment options, take control of your IRA wealth by diverting some or all of it to a self-directed IRA.

In a self-directed IRA, you are free to make nontraditional investments, as in CDs denominated in foreign currencies or stocks and bonds on foreign exchanges.

You can also buy and sell real estate in a self-directed IRA, or even use your money to invest in a business, though rules can be complicated to prevent self-dealing. You may not, for instance, own a controlling interest in a business in which you have invested your IRA, and personal funds can't be commingled with IRA funds for real estate purchases.[17]

Starting a self-directed IRA is straightforward. You will need to work through a custodial firm to disburse money and keep books. Your custodial firm is barred, however, from offering investment advice. To segregate risk, you may want to transfer only a portion of your IRA to the custodial firm.[18]

Table 9.1 includes a partial list of self-directed IRA custodian companies.

Convert to a Roth IRA?

If the bulk of your money is tied up in a 401(k) or 403(b) retirement account, this might be a good time to consider moving your assets to a Roth IRA. In a traditional IRA, you deposit pretax

Table 9.1   Custodian Companies for Self-Directed IRAs

Custodian	Location	Website
Entrust Administration, Inc.	various	entrustadministration.com
Equity Trust	Elyria, OH	trustetc.com
Guidant Financial Group	Bellevue, WA	guidantfinancial.com
IRA Resources Inc.	La Jolla, CA	iraresources.com
IRA Services Trust	San Carlos, CA	iraservices.com
Lincoln Trust	Denver, CO	lincolntrustco.com
Pensco Trust	San Francisco, CA	pensco.com
Polycomp Administrative Services	Roseville, CA	polycomp.net
Sterling Trust	Waco, TX	sterling-trust.com
Trust Administration Services Corp.	Carlsbad, CA	exeter1031.com

Source: Compiled by author.

dollars, but pay taxes on the entire amount upon withdrawal. With a Roth IRA, you make your contribution with post-tax dollars, but pay no further taxes on withdrawal.

Given current government spending, you can bet that future tax rates will be far higher than current tax rates. If your portfolio value is depressed, you may find it cheaper to pay taxes and penalties now and move your current IRA to a Roth.

The Roth IRA offers advantages to both young and old. For young or unemployed workers, it makes sense to convert your account now while you're in a 10 or 15 percent tax bracket. And for those concerned about passing on a nest egg, you've already paid taxes on your Roth IRA, so it passes tax free to a beneficiary.[19]

Running the Numbers

Does it make sense for you to convert your traditional IRA to a Roth IRA? MSN Money offers a simple way to run the numbers, with a web-based calculator that allows you to run different inflation and tax scenarios: http://money.msn.com/retirement/roth-ira-conversion-calculator.aspx

When Not to Convert to a Roth IRA

Despite the advantages of a Roth IRA, some potential transferees should think twice about doing a conversion. If you're 58 or older, a conversion seldom makes sense because you will be paying taxes on your IRA balance now in the hopes that portfolio growth will more than make up the difference in the future—a dicey proposition. The same logic applies if you're in a high tax bracket and the conversion will take a big bite out of your IRA balance.[20]

If on retirement you anticipate moving from a high-tax state like California or New York to a low-tax state like Texas or Nevada, your new lower tax bracket may obliterate any gains from changing over your Roth IRA. And if you plan to leave a large amount of your estate to charity, stick with a traditional IRA. That way neither you nor the charity will be taxed.[21]

Key Points

- Most Americans have significant wealth sequestered in IRAs and other retirement accounts that are closely tied to the health of the general economy.
- If you're stuck in an IRA, commodity mutual funds offer one way to hedge against inflation.
- U.S. Treasury bonds are no longer the safe investments they were in the past.
- TIPS are Treasury bonds indexed to inflation—but the government inflation numbers are highly manipulated, making the investment dubious.
- A self-directed IRA will give you more control over your retirement investment options.
- Converting to a Roth IRA makes sense for some, especially the young, the unemployed, or those with depressed portfolio values.

Prepare for the Worst, but Expect the Best

It is simply prudent to prepare for the worst that an inflation-induced monetary crisis can throw at us. This doesn't mean we dig a hole in our backyard and sit in it, waiting for the apocalypse. But it also doesn't mean we dig a hole in our backyard and stick our head in it. While no one knows exactly what the future will bring, we are still privileged to be able to arrange our affairs to avoid some of the more obvious pitfalls the flood of loose dollars will bring.

Here are a few realities.

CHAPTER

10

Why Your Taxes Are Going Sky High

As entitlement and debt-financing costs overwhelm any attempt at a rational tax policy, the federal government is developing a voracious appetite for higher and higher taxes. A cornucopia of tax measures—including new taxes on businesses, taxes on capital gains, and a VAT tax added on to the income tax—will keep the government afloat another decade, but will drag down economic growth, further impoverishing the country. The prosperous America of the twentieth century will give way to an era of economic stagnation and overbearing government regulation.

The Numbers Speak for Themselves: Someone Has to Pay

One way to see why huge new taxes are on their way is to break down the growth of the national debt on a per-worker basis.

There are about 125 million nongovernment and thus non-taxpayer-paid workers in the U.S.[1] In 2008, the national debt was "only" $10 trillion, rising exponentially to $15.5 trillion by the end of 2011.[2] Dividing the national debt by the number of nongovernment, non-taxpayer-paid workers, we find that the national debt load per worker was $80,000 in 2008, *but $124,000 in 2011.*

That's an increase in $44,000 per nongovernment, non-taxpayer-paid worker in the last four years.

You know what an additional $44,000 in credit card debt would do to your personal finances. (Few of us would be so foolish as to add fifty percent to our personal indebtedness in four short years.) But, in essence, the pain you would never inflict on yourself is the pain the federal government is willfully inflicting on you— assuming you're stupid enough to be one of those nongovernment non-taxpayer-paid workers.

As Elmer Peterson observed, "A democracy . . . can only exist until the majority discovers it can vote itself largesse out of the public treasury. After that, the majority always votes for the candidate promising the most benefits."[3]

Say Goodbye to Bush Tax Cuts

Tax cuts instituted by President Bush—a generous array of tax breaks for middle-class Americans, including child care credits and relief from the alternative minimum tax—are set to expire at the end of December 2012.[4]

The Bush tax cuts have become an election year football. Republicans want to make the cuts permanent, but Democrats argue that the cuts unfairly favor "the rich"—couples earning more than $250,000 per year (individuals, $200,000).[5]

Since the deficit super committee went down in flames over disagreements over how to handle the Bush tax cuts, it seems unlikely that a lame duck Congress will resolve the issue. Congressional inaction means the cuts will expire, raising an additional $3.3 trillion in taxes for the government to spend over the decade that follows.[6] That works out to an extra $25,000 for each of the country's 134 million tax payers.[7]

Tax Cuts to Expire After Election

"Since the deficit super committee went down in flames over disagreements over how to handle the Bush tax cuts, it seems unlikely that a lame duck Congress will resolve the issue. Congressional inaction means the cuts will expire."

Deficit Lip Service: How to Fool Some of the People Some of the Time

With unemployment at stubborn, record highs and the public beginning to rebel on the government's spend, spend, spend policies, leaders of both parties have been using their rhetorical gifts to sound more fiscally responsible.

For instance, in his 2011 State of the Union speech, the president proposed to "freeze annual domestic spending for the next five years."[8] But *USA Today* offered this reality check: "Obama revised last year's proposal to freeze domestic spending, excluding Social Security, Medicare and Medicaid, defense, homeland security and veterans' programs. . . . But by exempting so much, the freeze would apply to only about $500 billion of a $3.8 trillion budget—'a fairly narrow part,' White House economic adviser Gene Sperling admits."[9]

President Obama *sounds* like he wants to be fiscally responsible: "Rather than fight the same tired battles that have dominated Washington for decades, it's time to try something new. Let's invest in our people without leaving them a mountain of debt. Let's meet our responsibility to the citizens who sent us here. Let's try common sense."[10] (But is that rhetoric or a serious attempt to address the nation's debt problem?)

And in the House of Representatives, the Republican Study Committee proposed a "Spending Reduction Act" that would cap certain spending at 2006 levels. Unfortunately, the proposal—even if passed by the Democratic Senate—would trim only a few discretionary items, leaving Medicare, Medicaid, and Social Security untouched.[11] (Guess where the biggest increases in spending are over the next decade? See Figure 10.1 for the answer.)

What are the chances that our politicians will turn lip service into action before the train goes off the track?

The Greek Road to Ruin

In a television interview for Thames TV "This Week," former U.K. Prime Minister Margaret Thatcher said, "Socialist governments traditionally do make a financial mess. They always run out of other

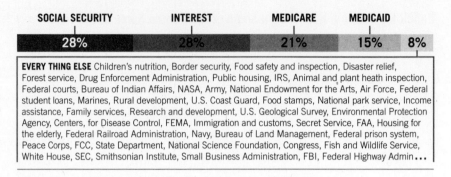

SOCIAL SECURITY	INTEREST	MEDICARE	MEDICAID	
28%	28%	21%	15%	8%

EVERY THING ELSE Children's nutrition, Border security, Food safety and inspection, Disaster relief, Forest service, Drug Enforcement Administration, Public housing, IRS, Animal and plant heath inspection, Federal courts, Bureau of Indian Affairs, NASA, Army, National Endowment for the Arts, Air Force, Federal student loans, Marines, Rural development, U.S. Coast Guard, Food stamps, National park service, Income assistance, Family services, Research and development, U.S. Geological Survey, Environmental Protection Agency, Centers, for Disease Control, FEMA, Immigration and customs, Secret Service, FAA, Housing for the elderly, Federal Railroad Administration, Navy, Bureau of Land Management, Federal prison system, Peace Corps, FCC, State Department, National Science Foundation, Congress, Fish and Wildlife Service, White House, SEC, Smithsonian Institute, Small Business Administration, FBI, Federal Highway Admin…

Figure 10.1   By 2020, Four Big Items Suck Up 92 Percent of Tax Dollars
Source: Money.com.

people's money."[12] No truer words have been spoken with regards to the Greek debt crisis.

It is a crisis that didn't have to happen. In the same year Margaret Thatcher made her perceptive comment, the right-wing military junta in Greece was replaced in democratic elections. The Greek economy was at the top of the growth list in the eurozone as foreign capital flooded the country after its 2001 euro entry. From 2000 to 2007, the annual rate of growth in Greece was 4.2 percent.[13]

Simultaneously, however, a series of left-leaning governments bought public support by running up large structural deficits to finance public sector jobs, pensions, and social benefits. The Maastricht criteria for EU admittance was debt below 60 percent of GDP and an annual deficit less than 3 percent. In Greece the numbers were 113 percent and 14 percent respectively.[14]

Le Nouvel Observateur comments that the chronic deficit problems in Greece are, like those of the United States, enshrined in the structure of the nation's finances. "For years the public debt ratio has never fallen below 100 percent of GDP [and] Greek tax revenues are insufficient to offset the spending," the newspaper observed. "Tax evasion is a national sport in Greece."[15]

Greece dealt with its spending problem in a creative way: Using Goldman Sachs and other banks, it devised ways to hide and misreport the actual level of its borrowing, thus giving investors a false idea of the safety of its bonds.[16] When the Papandreou government revised its deficit estimates from an estimated 6 percent to a more realistic figure double that amount (12.7%), investors lost confidence.[17] Interest rates shot up, reaching 152 percent in December 2011 for two-year bonds (see Figure 10.2).

With the threat of Greek default exposing the shaky foundation of the entire EU house, a series of increasingly draconian austerity packages were adopted by the government under pressure from the EU. Its limits on public-sector employee bonuses and pensions, along with huge increases in taxes, predictably brought chaos to the streets. A crowd of 70,000 workers converged on the square in front of Parliament, chanting slogans. "We just can't take it anymore," said municipal worker Nikos Anastasopoulos.[18]

Austerity measures enacted by the Greek parliament in February of 2012 brought more anarchists to the streets but failed to assuage the EU finance ministers trying to engineer a bailout, who want a

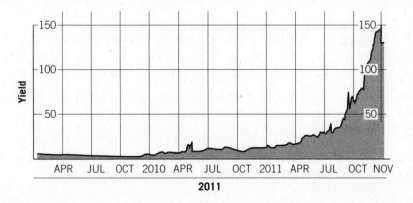

Figure 10.2   Interest Rate of Greek Two-Year Government Bonds Traded in the Secondary Market
Source: Bloomberg.

written pledge that the country's leaders will actually follow through on the programs if monies are disbursed.[19]

As Margaret Thatcher had predicted, Greece had run out of other people's money. Said former Federal Reserve Chairman Alan Greenspan: "Are they broke? Yeah. Are they going to resolve the issue in and of themselves? I can't see how."[20]

"New" Deficit Reduction Strategy: Taxes

With concerns mounting over the U.S. government's inability to get its spending under control ($1.267 trillion deficit in 2011, $1.57 trillion deficit in 2010, $1.4 trillion in 2009, etc.), the current administration has a new plan: taxes.[21, 22]

"I hope some of these folks who are hollering about deficits step up," President Obama said recently. "Because I'm calling their bluff."[23]

No, the President wasn't becoming a budget hawk, demanding a cutback in the growth of the federal budget, which the Congressional Budget Office (CBO) warns is on "an unsustainable path."[24] Instead, he was challenging his opponents to get on board with his solution: huge tax increases to help pay for the trillions of dollars in recent stimulus spending and unfunded healthcare subsidies.

And despite "hold-the-line" rhetoric in an election year, there are already signs that Republicans will find new taxes irresistible when compared to the alternative of actually cutting, say, defense spending. Republican Pat Toomey recently proposed raising taxes in exchange for lowering the top tax rate, for instance, and seemed content to allow a temporary payroll tax extension to disappear.[25, 26]

Coming Soon to Your Pocketbook: The Alternative Minimum Tax

The alternative minimum tax (AMT) is a tax trap originally intended to prevent people with very high incomes from paying little or no tax. Taxpayers are required to calculate their taxes showing what they would owe in the regular tax system, and then recalculate their taxes under a different system to capture at least a minimum tax.

When initiated under President Nixon, the system was designed to catch only a few hundred scofflaws making in excess of the then-outrageous $200,000 per year. By not indexing the tax, however, more and more middle-class people are forced to pay the alternative minimum tax. By 2010, the *New York Times* reports, "nearly 30 million taxpayers will be hit—among them, a staggering 94 percent of married filers who have children and make $75,000 to $100,000."[27]

Because every year more and more people get trapped by this alternative minimum tax, don't look for Congress or the administration to be in any hurry to repeal it soon.

Loophole: How to Turn a $700,000 Tax Bill into $10 Million Tax-Free Gift

If you have $1 million in your IRA, you may think you are leaving $1 million to your heirs. Not so. If you are in the maximum 45 percent estate tax bracket, $450,000 will immediately go to the tax man, not your heirs. Another $200,000 in taxes will be charged to your beneficiary, leaving just $350,000 of your original million.

Professor Rolf Auster of Florida International University outlines an ingenious loophole, however: Redesign your retirement plan to use its assets to purchase cash value life insurance. One million dollars should buy a $10 million policy. At your death, the insurance proceeds are paid—as nontaxable income—to your beneficiaries.

Specifically, the plan involves rolling over IRA funds into a 401(k) plan owned by a controlling entity. The 401(k) purchases a cash value life insurance policy as part of its investment plan. Upon your death, the named beneficiary receives the value of the life insurance tax free. Meanwhile, the policy holder may even borrow against the policy. (For a detailed discussion, read Professor Auster's discussion at http://www.allbusiness.com/personal-finance/retirement-estate-planning/637093-1.html)

The IRS, of course, abhors this loophole and is busy erecting a fence of regulations to keep you from passing your money to your heirs. In 2004, for instance, the Treasury Department issued guidance to cut down on deductions for "excess" life insurance.[28] If you do decide to pursue this strategy, consult a competent tax attorney.

How to Tax a Trillion Dollars

Jake Tapper, the ABC News senior White House correspondent, reports on Washington's plan to rake in $1 trillion in new taxes over the next 10 years. Here's his analysis:[29]

- Taxes on people making more than $250,000:
  $338 billion—Bush tax cuts expire
  $179 billion—Eliminate itemized deductions
  $118 billion—Capital gains tax hike
  Subtotal: $636 billion/10 years
- Taxes on businesses:
  $17 billion—Reinstate Superfund taxes
  $24 billion—Tax carried interest as income
  $5 billion—Codify "economic substance doctrine"
  $61 billion—Repeal LIFO
  $210 billion—International enforcement, reform deferral, other tax reform
  $4 billion—Information reporting for rental payments
  $5.3 billion—Excise tax on Gulf of Mexico oil and gas
  $3.4 billion—Repeal expensing of tangible drilling costs
  $62 million—Repeal deduction for tertiary injectants
  $49 million—Repeal passive loss exception for working interests in oil and natural gas properties
  $13 billion—Repeal manufacturing tax deduction for oil and natural gas companies
  $1 billion—Increase to seven years geological and geophysical amortization period for independent producers
  $882 million—Eliminate advanced earned income tax credit
  Subtotal: $353 billion/10 years

  Total: $636 billion + $353 billion = $989 billion/10 years

Your New Health Care Plan: Financed by Deception

Now that health care reform is the law of the land, look for huge new deficits. Here's the *Wall Street Journal's* take:

> Even though Medicare's unfunded liabilities are already about 2.6 times larger than the entire U.S. economy in 2008, Democrats are crowing that ObamaCare will cost "only" $871 billion

over the next decade while fantastically reducing the deficit by $132 billion, according to CBO.

Yet some 98% of the total cost comes after 2014 . . . and most of the taxes start in 2010. . . . Other deceptions include a new entitlement for long-term care that starts collecting premiums tomorrow but doesn't start paying benefits until late in the decade . . . payment cut[s] that won't happen but they remain in the bill to make the cost look lower . . . The truth is that no one really knows how much ObamaCare will cost because its assumptions on paper are so unrealistic.[30]

Baby Boom Legacy: Spiraling Entitlement Costs

The Government Accountability Office (GAO) has been warning for years that entitlement spending has been spiraling out of control (see Table 10.1). But is anyone in Washington listening? Here's an excerpt and table from their latest report:

Rising health care costs and the aging of the U.S. population have already begun to affect the federal budget, and their effect is expected to increase in coming decades as more members of the baby boom generation continue to retire and more people become eligible for federal health programs.

Table 10.1   Challenges Affecting the Federal Budget in the Near Term

2008	Oldest members of the baby boom generation became eligible for early Social Security retirement benefits.
2008	Medicare Hospital Insurance outlays exceeded cash income.
2010	Social Security runs first cash deficit in more than 25 years.
2011	Oldest members of the baby boom generation become eligible for Medicare.
2021	Debt held by the public under GAO's Alternative simulation exceeds the historical high reached in the aftermath of World War II.

For example, the Social Security program, which has historically run large cash surpluses that helped reduce the government's need to borrow from the public to finance other programs, paid more in benefits than it received in tax income in fiscal year 2010 for the first time in more than 25 years. CBO now projects that the program will continue running cash deficits into the future. This will contribute to the government's borrowing needs, putting additional pressure on the rest of the budget.

The report goes on to state, "The longer action to deal with the nation's long-term fiscal outlook is delayed, the greater the magnitude of the changes needed and the risk that the eventual changes will be disruptive and destabilizing."[31]

The Next Money-Grab: Value-Added Tax

The democratic socialist countries of Europe like France, Finland, and Germany have financed their extravagant social programs for decades through a value-added tax (VAT)—a national consumption tax on all goods and services. Value-added taxes are similar to sales taxes, with some adjustments to prevent taxing goods and services twice.

The VAT Tax Honeypot

"The VAT tax in France provides the government with 49.7 percent of its revenues. Standard VAT rates in European countries average around 20 to 25 percent."

The Obama administration's first White House Budget Director, Peter Orszag, was a London School of Economics–trained economist who floated the possibility of a "modest" 5 to 6 percent VAT here in the United States as a way to tackle the worrisome budget deficits.[32] Former Massachusetts governor and current Republican primary candidate Mitt Romney says he might consider a value-added tax.[33] And a PricewaterhouseCoopers LLP Report ("Tax Policy in a Deficit-Driven World") notes that the United States "is the only OECD

Table 10.2   Changes in VAT Rates over Time

	Rate When First Enacted	Current Rate	Top Marginal Income Tax Rate
Canada	7%	5%	46.4%
Denmark	9	25	59.7
France	13.6	19.6	45.8
Germany	10	19	47.5
Italy	12	20	44.9
Japan	3	5	50
Spain	12	16	43
Sweden	17.7	25	56.4
Switzerland	6.5	7.6	41.7
United Kingdom	8	17.5	50
United States	0	0	35*

*Federal rate, rising to 39.6% in 2013

Source: The *Wall Street Journal.*

country without a national-level value-added tax (VAT) on goods and services"—a "problem" fiscal commission member Andy Stern proposes to remedy with a 10 to 15 percent consumption tax.[34]

You can see the attraction for politicos: The VAT tax in France provides the government with 49.7 percent of its revenues.[35]

Standard VAT rates in European countries average around 20 to 25 percent (of course, when first enacted, the rates were closer to 10 to 15%).[36] (See Table 10.2).

Imagine tacking an extra 20 to 25 percent onto the cost of everything you buy.

Now imagine the drain that will be on middle-class household budgets and the damage such a tax would do to savings and to investments that actually produce jobs.

Tax Fig Leaf: Erroneous Economic Models

Politicians love Keynesian economics because it provides intellectual cover for doing what they love to do most: Spend money the government doesn't have.

In *The General Theory of Employment, Interest and Money,* published in the middle of the Great Depression in 1936, Keynes argued that increasing government spending can help drive an economy through a "multiplier effect"—an increase in economic output over and above the amount of money spent. In a downturn, Keynesians believe, the government should step-up spending aggressively in order to pump dollars into the system, theoretically putting the economy on amphetamines. Hence repeated calls by Paul Krugman—a *New York Times* columnist and Nobel laureate in economics—for bailouts and more bailouts. Evidence that Keynesian economic policies are failing (e.g., economic malaise and 9.1 percent unemployment after $3.27 trillion in stimulus spending) are simply chalked up to insufficient government spending.[37, 38, 39]

"If you're serious about fiscal responsibility," Krugman said in a Bloomberg Television "Street Smart" interview, "you should not be saying, 'Let's skimp on aid to the economy in the middle of a financial crisis.' . . . The most effective things you can do, in terms of actual bang for the buck, is actually having the federal government go out and hire people."[40]

To Keynesians, it doesn't matter what the people actually do— Keynes suggested that hiring workers to dig holes in the ground would increase both employment and the output of goods and services. You can see the appeal to politicians, who get to allocate that wash of federal dollars showering down from Washington to pay the ditch-diggers. They not only are "giving" workers jobs, they are altruistically keeping the economy going, and without any negative consequences.

Keynesians forget that even Keynes argued that the workers should be paid out of government *savings*—not *borrowings,* as in the current case. When the federal government borrows money to pay ditch-diggers in make-work projects, it is creating a debt that will become a drag on future generations as they struggle to repay it. That means future tax increases.

Not only that, the government stimulus spending drives up wages; a private employer who wants to hire a ditch digger will have to match whatever arbitrary rate the government is handing out that day. Keynesian stimulus spending ideas ignore the inefficiency of the state bureaucracy in allocating and spending capital.

Says Allan Meltzer, a professor of public policy at Carnegie Mellon University, "The estimated cost of new jobs in President Obama's latest jobs bill is at least $200,000 per job, based on administration estimates of the number of jobs and their cost. . . . Once the subsidies end, the jobs disappear—but the bonds that financed them remain and must be serviced."[41]

Ouch! Economic Medicine That Works

There is an alternative to Keynesian economics: the so-called "Austrian school," which emphasizes business cycles and the dangers of wrong-headed government economic meddling.

Why don't more policy makers gravitate to Austrian school solutions? The Austrian school believes the quickest way out of a recession is to let the malfeasants feel the full pain of their bad decisions. Here, for instance, is an Austrian school solution for an economic downturn (by Mark Thornton, senior resident fellow at the Ludwig von Mises Institute):

- Allow liquidation of bankrupt firms and debt (no bailouts).
- Allow prices to fall (no monetary inflation).
- Do not prop up employment (no stimulus).
- Give no assurances against failure (no nationalizations of GSEs or expanding FDIC coverage).
- Do not subsidize unemployment (no extending of unemployment insurance).
- Do not discourage "hoarding," i.e., saving.[42]

If you were a politico, which would you choose: easy Keynesian largesse, in which you can pretend to be doing something constructive even if it doesn't work—or hard Austrian medicine, which will taste bad at first but will help the patient recover quickly?

I thought so.

Expect a long Keynesian hangover in the form of more regulations, slow economic growth, mounting deficits, and—of course—higher taxes.

Why the United States Will Never Be the Same Again

The current generation of leaders is rapidly destroying the underpinnings of financial prosperity and economic production that is the legacy of "America's Century."

The middle class is on the ropes. Sixty-one percent of Americans "always or usually" live paycheck to paycheck, up from 43 percent in 2007. Forty-three percent have less than $10,000 saved for retirement. There were 1.3 million bankruptcies in 2011—up almost 30 percent from 2008 for the third year in a row.[43, 44] And though the nominal unemployment rate has been slowly declining, the reason seems to be that "there may be three million long-term unemployed people who are currently not being counted by the Labor Department because they have simply given up looking for work."[45]

Manufacturing in the United States has stagnated as factories have moved offshore. The *New York Times* reports that the United States has lost about one-third of its manufacturing jobs in the last decade—putting five million workers out on the street.[46] The goods and services deficit in 2011 was over $550 billion dollars.[47] An M.I.T. commission investigating the state of American manufacturing concluded "we need to create 17 to 20 million jobs in the coming decade to recover from the current downturn and meet upcoming job needs."[48]

U.S. economic power in the world is in decline. Patrick Buchanan points out that

> The United States began the century producing 32% of the world's gross domestic product. We ended the decade producing 24%. No nation in modern history, save for the late Soviet Union, has seen so precipitous a decline in relative power in a single decade.[49]

According to a consensus report prepared by the National Intelligence Council, the U.S. growth rate is likely to drop to an anemic 1.5 percent through 2030. "Seen as a country on the down slide, the United States is both incapable of leading and disinclined to lead," wrote one contributor.[50]

Simply put, America's Century—which brought enormous innovation, increased social freedom for the poor and minorities, achieved a high standard of living for the middle class, and helped stabilize the world economic order—is about to come to an abrupt end as the dollar collapses under the weight of decades of debt and mismanagement. The structural changes in entitlement programs needed to make them viable are politically unpalatable and thus unlikely to be implemented. Prepare for a future of high taxes, stagnant growth, rapid inflation, and broken government promises.

Key Points

- Federal debt per nongovernment worker is up $44,000 in four years.
- Both parties pay lip service to debt reduction, but the amount of public debt keeps rising.
- Expect a tidal wave of new taxes over the next decade to help pay for out-of-control government spending.
- The GAO warns of "disruptive and destabilizing" deficits in health care, Medicare, and Social Security costs.
- Keynesian economic policies provide a convenient excuse for politicians to shovel money at economic problems, but may actually be making the economy worse.
- America's influence in the world is waning as growth of the U.S. economy slows to a crawl.

CHAPTER

11

Look for the Warning Signs

The demise of the dollar is already under way, as policies set by the Federal Reserve work to push the dollar lower. Officials believe, of course, that they can manage an orderly dollar decline, but the *dénouement* may come swiftly as nervous traders push the United States into a Greek-style bond crisis, bankrupting the country overnight. Wage and price controls, restrictions on gold and wealth imports, and rapid inflation will follow. In the end, the elderly and poor will suffer the most as government entitlement promises are proved hollow.

The Warning Signs of an Imminent Currency Collapse

The onset of hyperinflation can be compared to the onset of an avalanche: While the exact moment of the wave of devastation is unknowable, warning signs will increasingly abound in the moments leading up to the triggering event. Just as avalanches are caused by a stress on the snowpack, inflation is triggered by stress on a currency. The weight of falling snow—like the weight of dollars rained down by Ben Bernanke's helicopter—gradually accumulates to massive proportions. At that point even a small disturbance can tip the balance to let loose catastrophic destruction.

A massive, economically-unjustified increase in the amount of dollars in circulation is the prerequisite for the hyperinflation avalanche. The Federal Reserve has been busily preparing the slopes

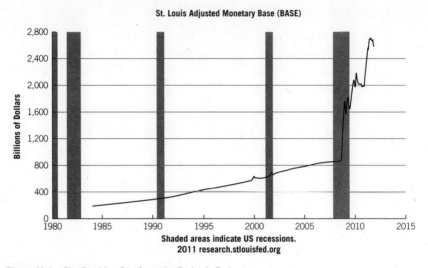

St. Louis Adjusted Monetary Base (BASE)

Shaded areas indicate US recessions.
2011 research.stlouisfed.org

Figure 11.1   The Smoking Gun from the St. Louis Fed

Source: Federal Reserve Bank of St. Louis.

for this event through its unprecedented increase in the dollar's monetary base (see Figure 11.1).

Ironically, in 2006 Richard G. Anderson—the vice president of the Federal Reserve Bank of St. Louis—explicitly warned of the hyperinflation danger this kind of "hockey stick" growth in the money supply portends:

> So long as the public willingly holds additional [monetary] base money, the central bank is able to purchase assets and expand its size. Historically, this has tempted governments with weak fiscal discipline to utilize the central bank as a purchaser-of-last-resort for government debt when private capital markets are unreceptive, often leading to hyper-inflation.[1]

In Operation Twist, the Fed is already purchasing its own government debt, and the public is increasingly becoming unwilling to absorb additional dollars. IAS 29 Financial Reporting Standards point to five characteristics of a hyperinflationary environment:

1. The general population prefers to keep its wealth in nonmonetary assets or in a relatively stable foreign currency.

Amounts of local currency held are immediately invested to maintain purchasing power.

2. The general population regards monetary amounts not in terms of the local currency but in terms of a relatively stable foreign currency. Prices may be quoted in that currency.

3. Sales and purchases on credit take place at prices that compensate for the expected loss of purchasing power during the credit period, even if the period is short.

4. Interest rates, wages, and prices are linked to a price index.

5. The cumulative inflation rate over three years approaches, or exceeds, 100 percent.[2]

Investment flows, the price of gold, interest in TIPS, and contracts and benefits linked to the consumer price index (CPI) all give evidence of an increase in momentum in points 1 through 4; point 5 awaits a triggering event.

According to Allan Meltzer, a professor at the Tepper School of Business, Carnegie Mellon University, that triggering event "will be either a sustained increase in bank lending or a large increase in Fed purchases of government debt."[3] When all the conditions are in place, the onset of runaway inflation will, like the onset of an avalanche, be swift. The triggering event might be almost anything—rumors of war, the failure of a large bank, or rising bond prices that suddenly begin to spike.

The Final Countdown

"When all the conditions are in place, the onset of runaway inflation will, like the onset of an avalanche, be swift. The triggering event might be almost anything—rumors of war, the failure of a large bank, or rising bond prices that suddenly begin to spike."

With financial markets around the world linked in an intricate electronic web by the Internet, traders will begin to dump dollars and U.S. government debt—at first slowly, then in an ever-accelerating downward sell-off. The crisis might even begin overseas, after American markets have closed for the day, spreading from markets in Singapore and Hong Kong across the globe to Amsterdam and London.

By the time New York exchanges finally open, a full scale panic will be under way. Prices of gold, oil, and other commodities will soar while stocks and bonds prices fall off a cliff, pushing down market indexes by 30, 40, 50 percent or more. After a few hours of chaos, the federal government will step in to stop trading.

By late afternoon, lines will form at banks and ATMs as it begins to dawn on the average citizen that their money is not safe. The Federal Reserve will attempt a massive program of buying up U.S. Treasuries, but this will actually have a negative effect in foreign markets. Currency controls will be put in place and border control agents will be watching for the new smugglers—Americans trying to get their wealth out of the country.

Virtually overnight, the American economy will degrade to that of a third-world country. Store shelves will empty and prices soar, with fewer and fewer sellers willing to accept American dollars for anything of value. The flow of oil from around the world will cease and gasoline will become impossible to obtain.

Exchanges will be conducted by barter for liquor, cigarettes, and gold and silver coins. Massive amounts of valuables will be smuggled south to Mexico and north to Canada, where people can still pay for them in currency that means something. Meanwhile, rioting and martial law may ensue in parts of the country as officials struggle to regain control.

Is the U.S. Government Secretly Engineering a Weak Dollar?

"The Federal Reserve believes that a strong and stable dollar is both in American interests and in the interest of the global economy," Federal Reserve Chairman Ben Bernanke said in 2011.[4]

That's the official line. But evidence abounds that the Fed *intends* to weaken the dollar.

First, in January 2011, the White House hosted a low-key dinner with Chinese President Hu Jintao, where, it is rumored, the United States and China reached a secret agreement to let the yuan rise against the dollar.[5, 6] Whether by design or coincidence, the dollar took a precipitous dive shortly thereafter—as shown in Figure 11.2.

CNY per 1 USD

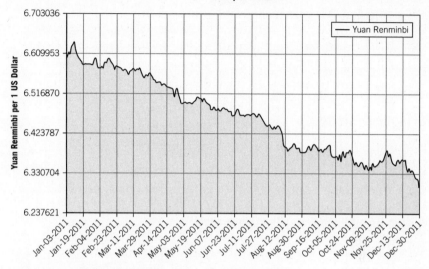

Figure 11.2   Dollar Dive against Yuan: Design or Coincidence?

Source: eXchangeRate.com.

And then there's the actions of the Fed, which has repeatedly extended dollar swap lines to central banks of the EC, Canada, Britain, Switzerland, and Japan—essentially giving an unlimited bailout to foreign banks short of dollars.[7] Why? Contrarian investor Mike Norman explains.

> The Fed doesn't have to do this. Central banks of these respective countries and trade zones could provide dollars by selling their domestic currencies and buying dollars in the foreign exchange markets. But, heaven forbid, that would mean weakening their currencies and making the dollar stronger.[8]

Other actions by the Federal Reserve also point to a concerted effort to push down the value the of the dollar: showering the country with trillions in stimulus money, buying down toxic debt, and purposely keeping interest rates near zero percent. From the policy maker's point of view, a weak dollar helps boost American exports (in line with the president's initiatives in this area) and knocks down the value of the country's obligations by forcing creditors to accept a devalued dollar.

But as *London Telegraph* commentator Liam Halligan observes, the danger of this game is that it could backfire:

> If "the rope slips" and a steady dollar decline turns into free fall . . . a rapid "unwinding" could cause major losses at financial institutions, posing renewed systemic dangers. Far from being a safe haven, the dollar is the likely source of the next financial crisis.[9]

Words are one thing, actions another. So despite the blathering of officials like Ben Bernanke and Treasury Secretary Timothy Geithner, the United States wants a dollar that is heading down, not up.

How to Be a Billionaire—Zimbabwe-Style

When Zimbabwe was the British colony of Rhodesia, it had reasonably stable finances and was a net food exporter, rich in natural resources.[10] Decades of government socialism and the tyrannical reign of Robert Mugabe brought the economy to ruin. The inflation rate—already over 30 percent a decade ago—shot up in the summer of 2008 to an astronomical 89,700,000,000,000,000,000,000 percent, bringing ruin on its citizens.[11] The Zimbabwe central bank issued, in quick succession, a series of ever-larger banknotes which bought less and less. (Zimbabwe's worthless 100 trillion banknotes [$100,000,000,000] have become a currency curiosity, and enjoy a brisk trade on eBay; see Figure 11.3.)

Figure 11.3   Model for the United States?

Moses Chikomba's $50 billion monthly salary would buy just two bars of soap—or only one if he delayed spending for a day. "We are all billionaires who can afford nothing," he told a *London Times* reporter.[12] Once a beautiful country, Zimbabwe's economy has been ruined by three decades of gross corruption, misrule, and mismanagement. Could Zimbabwe-style economics come to the United States?

Is the United States the Next Greece?

Alan Greenspan, former chairman of the Federal Reserve, points out that there are limits on the amount a country can expect to borrow to finance debt—even if the country is the United States. While the United States is free to create as many dollars as it wishes to meet its Treasury bond obligations, it cannot control the interest rate investors are willing to pay for the bonds.

"We cannot count on foreigners to finance our current account deficit indefinitely," he says.

With federal debt surging from $5.5 trillion to $8.6 trillion in just a year and a half, the government risks becoming another Greece, where over-the-top spending spooked international investors. As that scenario unfolded, the cost of government borrowing went through the roof, causing massive job cutbacks, riots in the street by federal employees, and a currency crisis that may yet cause the fall of the euro.

"In the past decade the U.S. has been unable to cut any federal spending programs of significance," comments Greenspan. "Only politically toxic cuts or rationing of medical care, a marked rise in the eligible age for health and retirement benefits, or significant inflation, can close the deficits."[13]

With U.S. lawmakers unable or unwilling to prioritize tough spending choices, "significant inflation"—along with Greek-style discord as government workers and entitlement wards take it to the street—seems the most likely outcome. Opines Martin Kress in *Weimar Exhumed*:

> If foreign debt buyers desert a government and that government's debt-bonds can attract only one buyer—its own central

bank, expect the value of their currency to collapse. The government will not be able to print and distribute money fast enough to stay ahead of the death spiral.[14]

Operation Double-Twist?

"If foreign debt buyers desert a government and that government's debt-bonds can attract only one buyer—its own central bank, expect the value of their currency to collapse."

Got Gold?

The same Emergency Banking Act of 1933 that closed the banks also authorized the Secretary of the Treasury to order citizens to deliver any gold that they possessed to the Treasury in return for "any other form of coin or currency coined or issued under the laws of the United States"—under threat of 10 years imprisonment and $10,000 fines for each day of noncompliance.[15]

Nor was 1933 the last time the U.S. government has seized legal control of private citizens' assets. In 1968, Democratic President Lyndon Johnson placed mandatory controls on foreign investments and loans made overseas.[16] And in January 1980, silver investors were hit with a rule by the board of commodities exchange, limiting their trading to "liquidation only."[17]

The point is that desperate governments can use their arbitrary power to restrict private owners from accessing or using their money. The complete computerization of the banking system now makes privacy almost impossible, and guarantees the government an easy mechanism to shut you out from your accounts.

Wage and Price Controls

When inflation does begin to get out of control, a favorite way for governments to "do something" is to institute wage and price controls. Wage and price controls have been used throughout history—from the Roman Empire to the French Revolution to World War I America—in a futile attempt to maintain the value of rapidly deteriorating currency.

The Franklin Roosevelt administration created the Office of Price Administration to unsuccessfully try to control spiraling prices during World War II.[18] On August 15, 1971, with inflation rising "only" at a 4 to 6 percent rate, President Richard Nixon imposed wage and price controls. Originally intended to be a 90-day freeze, the temporary freeze became nearly three years of price and wage control attempts.[19] Not until the price controls were removed in late 1974 did inflation actually come under control. (See Figure 11.4).

Even when freezes are successful in holding down prices, the laws of economics dictate that under price controls sellers will begin to hold back goods from the marketplace, resulting in shortages. Hence 60 years of rent control in New York City has led to severe housing shortages and increased prices on uncontrolled apartments.[20]

Price controls can also be seen as an attempt by a government to force citizens to accept devalued paper money at its face rate as legal tender. If the government owes you a $10,000 tax refund, it can offer as payment paper money with a $10,000 face value, even if inflation has made the buying power of that money only $5,000. Refuse to accept this "legal tender" and you will go to jail.

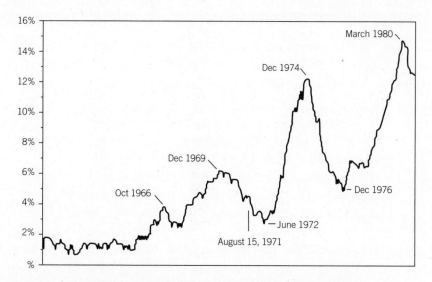

Figure 11.4   Effect of Nixon Wage and Price Controls: CPI Inflation Rate, 1960–1980

Source: The Econ Review (http://www.econreview.com).

Despite their proven ineffectiveness, expect wage and price controls to be part of any ongoing financial crisis. That way, political demagogues can allow inflation to perform their dirty work while claiming to be doing something for the average man.

The Lesson of the Russian Grandmothers

In a state of monetary breakdown, expect disruptions in government payments. Even five years after the breakup of Soviet communism, Russia remained in a state of anarchy. "The pensioners have nothing to live on," said one woman. "I worked for 41 years, on the Boyevik collective farm. It's painful to work so hard and be left with nothing." Only 18 percent of Russians reported they were receiving a regular paycheck, and many had not been paid for months. In Noginsk, one retiree's pension of 400 rubles a month was cut in half by the 1998 devaluation, and her son, on whom she relied for assistance, hadn't been paid himself in 5 months.[21]

Social Security, Hyperinflation Style

"I worked for 41 years, on the Boyevik collective farm. It's painful to work so hard and be left with nothing."

Eric Kraus, managing director of Anyatta Capital and a personal witness to the collapse of the Soviet Union, called pensioners "the true losers in 'Russia's Historic Transformation.'"

> After a lifetime toiling in a system they had been brought up to believe in . . . [they] were suddenly and inexplicably left destitute, with their six-dollar pensions inadequate to purchase food, medicine, or warm clothes—disoriented in an alien, hostile new world; coal miners unpaid for 18 months; teachers and doctors who had watched their safe, orderly worlds crumble.[22]

In the aftermath of the Soviet collapse, millions of people were left in total poverty. Across the entire country, paychecks ran from 3 to 8 months behind, and there were equally long delays in paying pensions, family subsidies, and even health subsidies for those affected by Chernobyl.

The new Russian government taxed corporate profits at over 90 percent, driving businessmen to take steps to send their money and families out of the country. With an inflation rate of 25 to 30 percent a month, even those workers who were paid couldn't feed their families. For ordinary people, everything they had been saving for during their entire life simply melted away in a few weeks of hyperinflation. Crime took off, and Moscow streets were filled with Russian grandmothers hawking apples in a desperate bid to survive.

Don't look for the government to keep up with welfare, Social Security, or other federal payments in the event of a national bankruptcy.

Key Points

- The Federal Reserve is massively increasing the dollar supply without a corresponding increase in economic activity, setting the stage for hyperinflation.
- As the tipping point is reached, spiking bond prices or another unforeseen event will initiate a rush to dump dollars.
- Wage and price controls—though historically ineffective— are likely to return as a way of attempting to maintain the value of the dollar as legal tender.
- Access to financial accounts may be restricted during the crisis, and new regulations may attempt to confiscate gold or other forms of wealth.
- Retirees, the poor, and the sick will suffer most from the currency meltdown, as benefits are paid in increasingly worthless dollars.

Looking Up While Hunkering Down

Whether the monetary breakdown of the U.S. dollar proves to be a slow-motion train wreck or a quick disaster, it can't hurt to be prepared. Some low-key ways to get started: Prepare a stay bag for emergencies, keep some coins at home for barter, protect your privacy from snoops, and develop a marketable hobby skill. Hopefully you've already started inflation-proofing your portfolio; become even more self-sufficient by going off the grid, and add your voice to the community of people trying to get the country back on sound fiscal track.

Speak Out

Although more and more our political elites seem to exist in a bubble impenetrable by fiscal reality, they depend on the complacency of the populace to allow their self-serving and foolish deeds to go unpunished.

Make yourself a voice to be reckoned with. Let your representatives and senators hear from you loudly and often when voting on bills that will affect your future and the future of your children. Politicos will blow off a single letter, e-mail, fax, or phone call. But if they are inundated with hundreds, thousands, or hundreds of thousands of communications, their arrogance can be slowed and stopped.

Hold your representatives' feet to the fire. Let them hear from you when you are displeased. Turn yourself into the nagging voice of their conscience. They need a nudge to do what they know they ought to be doing.

Another Way to Multiply Your Voice

Join with other like-minded citizens to protect your interests and amplify your voice. Consider working from within to set the right agenda and to choose viable candidates who will protect the interests of the U.S. dollar and the U.S. middle class.

For mainstream Republicans and Democrats, a trip to party websites will detail races to follow, candidates' statements, ways to donate, and volunteer opportunities.

The American Tea Party Movement is a conservative (but nonpartisan) group that organizes demonstrations and informational events around the country to try to pressure politicos to do the right thing. Despite unprincipled attempts to label the Tea Party as "racist," the grassroots uprising was highly effective in changing the tenor of the debate in the lead-up to the 2010 midterm elections.

The Libertarian Party campaigns on the slogan of "smaller government, lower taxes, more freedom." Although not powerful at the polls, libertarians have become increasingly successful at injecting Libertarian ideas into public policy debates—witness the surge in popularity of Ron Paul in the 2012 Republican primaries.

And if your taste in protests runs to the far left, find a local park to occupy with the Occupy Movement, which came to prominence in September of 2011 with its encampment in New York City's financial district. According to AdBusters.org, which was instrumental in getting the protests started, Occupy Wall Street is a "leaderless people-powered movement for democracy." (What this new "democracy" would look like appears to be an open question.)

Develop a Necessary Skill

If political pressure fails to bring the dollar back from the brink, take the next step and develop your economic value for the hard times sure to follow. Even during an economic crisis, people need to eat, to move around, to drink clean water, and to obtain medical care. Certain skills are proven to be in high demand during severe downturns and catastrophes:

- Accounting (making every penny work will be a full-time job for most businesses)

- Car/motorcycle mechanic (think of Cuba—land of 50-year-old running cars)
- Chemical/mechanical/hydraulic engineer (someone has to get the infrastructure working again)
- Clergy (broken spirits will need hope to mend)
- Debt collector, tax collector, foreclosure specialist, enforcer (creditors will want their money)
- Doctor/nurse/EMT/veterinarian (people will pay dearly for health)
- Electrician/electronics/computer tech (infrastructure on a small scale)
- Farmer/gardener (give us this day our daily bread)
- Heavy equipment operator (from farms to industry, earth will have to be moved)
- Law enforcement (tough times need tough crime fighters)
- Pilots, engineers, boat captains (highly skilled professionals for transporting people and things)
- Plumbers, heating techs (water, sanitation, and heat will always be in need)
- Tailor (clothing must last longer)
- Trader/distributor/business executive (bartering will be a way of life)
- Vice industries (sex, alcohol, drugs, and gambling—always a fallback when times are tough)

Position yourself now by developing your skills in these sellable areas as a hobby or second business. Learn to garden, create a small-scale energy project, or volunteer as an emergency medical technician. You'll have fun and save money while learning a new trade.

Start an Export Business

Exporting American goods is a huge business. According to the U.S. Department of Commerce, American companies exported over $1.28 trillion of merchandise in 2010, up from around $750 million a decade before.[1] As the dollar declines in value, exports will surge because American goods will be bargain priced.

Toilets, gourmet food, telephone poles, navigational aids, pet food—possible export niches are endless. You are limited only

Table 12.1   Export Trends

Share of Total U.S. Manufacturing Exports	2000	2005	2010	Compound Annual Growth Rate 2000–2010
Growing Sectors				
Chemical, plastic, rubber, and petroleum products	16.1%	19.4%	27.00%	+9.5%
Food, beverages, and tobacco	4.7	4.1	5.9	+6.3
Other manufactured products	15.0	16.5	17.8	+5.8
Transportation equipment	18.8	20.0	18.5	+3.8
Machinery, including appliances and electrical equipment	17.2	16.7	16.5	+3.6
Shrinking Sectors				
Computers and electronic products	25.1%	21.0%	12.7%	−2.8%
Textiles and apparel	3.1	2.4	1.7	−2.1

Source: New York Times.

by your ability to bring together a willing seller and needful buyer. Fastest growing export sectors include chemical and petroleum products, transportation equipment, and machinery. Exports of apparel and computing products are on the downswing (see Table 12.1).

To be successful as an exporter you need to find appealing products that set your business apart from your competitors. Target a specific economic segment (electrical generation, medical) and get started by becoming an export management company—finding buyers for goods manufactured by American companies. As you develop contacts, expand your export line to include other products and services that extend your niche.

Prepare a "Stay Bag"

Long disruptions in the electrical supply may become a way of life as the American economy begins to resemble that of a third-world country. Living without power for days at a time can be inconvenient, even life threatening, depending on the length of the outage and the season of the year. Heating, water, refrigeration, as well as lights, telephone, and Internet service all depend on electricity.

An Ounce of Caution . . .

"Even if you're not worried about economic disruptions to electrical services, it's prudent to prepare a 'stay bag' if only to guard against natural disasters."

Even if you're not worried about economic disruptions to electrical services, it's prudent to prepare a "stay bag" if only to guard against natural disasters. A rare October snowstorm dumped as much as 32 inches of snow in the Northeast in 2011, leaving 1.6 million people without power for days.[2] Hurricane Irene was even more disastrous, leaving eight dead in its wake and 2 million without power.[3] A stay bag enables you to "camp" in your house, staying safe until utilities can restore power.

What should go into your stay bag? Here are some suggestions drawn from FEMA and other disaster-preparedness experts:

- Water. One gallon per person per day. Municipal or private pumps can shut down during a power emergency, affecting water flow to your tap. If the water is still running when the lights go out, stopper and fill your bathtub to provide an immediate reserve. In winter, keep your faucets dribbling to prevent pipes from freezing.
- Water purification equipment. If you have to drink from runoff, melted snow, or from other questionable supplies, purify your water before drinking. Bring the water to a rolling boil for one minute if you still have a working stove, or use a water filtration hand pump (available from camping suppliers) to filter enough water to drink. According to the Washington State Department of Health, liquid chlorine bleach (like Clorox or Purex) can treat water in a pinch. Mix thoroughly and allow to stand 60 minutes before consuming. Table 12.2 shows a chart of recommended treatment amounts.
- Food. Have enough canned or packaged food on hand to weather three days without power. A propane camp stove such as those made by Coleman or Optimus can be used for light cooking in a well-ventilated room.

Table 12.2   Treating Water with a 5 to 6 Percent Chlorine Bleach Solution

Volume of Water to Be Treated	Treating Clear/Cloudy Water: Bleach Solution to Add	Treating Cloudy, Very Cold, or Surface Water: Bleach Solution to Add
1 quart/1liter	3 drops	5 drops
1/2 gallon/2 quarts/2 liters	5 drops	10 drops
1 gallon	1/8 teaspoon	1/4 teaspoon
5 gallons	1/2 teaspoon	1 teaspoon
10 gallons	1 teaspoon	2 teaspoons

Source: Department of Health Pub 821-031 Revised Jan. 2009.

- Lighting. An LED camping lantern and flashlights will provide general illumination. LEDs use power more efficiently than conventional flashlight bulbs and thus extend battery life. Spare alkaline batteries should be kept handy and rotated so that you have them when you need them. LED flashlights that work by solar power or by cranking a dynamo are available on Amazon and via eBay—though even these rely on small batteries to store a charge. Bags of tea lights—candles in individual tin holders—require no batteries and should be stored with a butane lighter to fire them up.
- Clothing and sleeping bags. Presumably you already have winter clothing on hand for everyday use. Long underwear, hats, scarves, and gloves can keep you warm if the heat is out in your home. For sleeping, you will need multiple blankets, comforters, or sleeping bags.
- Heat. For heat consider a propane heater, such as the "Buddy" line produced by Mr. Heater (http://www.mrheater.com/ProductFamily.aspx?catid=41). Running off bottled propane gas, these heaters are portable and both easier to use and safer than previous-generation kerosene heaters, which can cause fire or fumes if bumped. Buddy heaters have a low oxygen safety shut-off switch and can be used indoors with windows cracked for ventilation. The heaters are small enough to carry and will keep a medium-sized room warm in subfreezing temperatures.
- Refrigeration. Refrigerators are insulated and will keep food cold for a day or more if you avoid opening them more than

necessary. Perishable food can be stored outside under snow or in the corner of a cool basement.

- Communications. A landline phone has its own wiring and is much more likely to work during a power outage. VOIP (Internet) phone service will go out with the electrical power, as will most likely your Internet connection itself. Cell phones may or may not work (and can enable you to connect to the Internet if working, if your cell is able to create its own hot spot.) If relying on cell phones or laptops, dim the screen brightness to conserve power.
- A portable radio. Battery, solar, or crank operated, it will provide weather and news updates and local stations may even connect community members with each other during an emergency. During the Northridge earthquake in Los Angeles in 1994, many Angelenos sat out the night in their cars listening to radio broadcasts of the unfolding chaos. Power inverters can turn your car's power outlet (i.e., cigarette lighter) into 120 volt AC, enabling you to recharge cell batteries. (Run the car while using the charger to avoid draining your car battery.)

Tangibles to Keep at Home

In a severe economic crisis, expect shortages and breakdowns of delivery of goods and services. Shortages of natural gas, milk, and other food products followed Argentina's surge in inflation, and service stations around Buenos Aires were ordered to stop pumping gas as a way of controlling energy supplies.

To make your life more bearable during a period of social breakdown, you will want to stockpile some supplies. Food, water, clothing, medical, and energy needs are your first line of defense. Keep your pantry filled with nonperishable food, using and replacing it to keep your supplies fresh in times of plenty. Each spring, buy a supply of viable vegetable seeds. Have a cache of blankets, pillows, sleeping bags, and warm clothing. Water pressure may become unreliable or water may become unsafe to drink in certain circumstances, and a family of four will need at least 125 gallons to survive one month. As noted above, Clorox bleach can disinfect water in a pinch.

Medicine, medical supplies, and how-to and survival guides all could prove handy in an extended societal breakdown, as could a hunting rifle and ammunition. Don't neglect hygiene items like soap, garbage bags, toothpaste, and toilet paper. A radio will keep you connected and informed. To get around economically when gas supplies are tight, consider a small scooter or motorcycle. Of course, bicycles use zero fuel and are simple to keep in repair.

Buy a small safe for your valuables. In it can go a store of coins and bills. Stockpile both American currency (it may still have some value for someone) and a selection of gold and silver coins. Include some recognizable pre-1964 U.S. silver coins. You may also want to stockpile barter items likely to be in short supply: tobacco, ammo, razors, candles, tools, nuts and bolts, cotton diapers, condoms, and kitchen utensils all have proven high value in areas of scarcity.

Hopefully, the need for such tangibles will never come to pass, and a slow-motion rolling catastrophe (i.e., slow erosion of your wealth combined with ever more restrictive laws and regulations) is more likely than a complete societal breakdown. So pick and choose from these suggestions as you see fit.

Whisky and Pot: Your Depression Friends

When oil price shocks and the cost of importing grain led to the bankruptcy and subsequent collapse of the Soviet Union in 1991, the rate of poverty sharply increased, with the World Bank estimating that up to half the population was living below the poverty line.[4, 5]

Alcoholism—always a problem in Soviet Russia, where the rate of alcohol consumption is about double that of the United States[6]—shot up 115 percent as inflation took hold and life expectancies plummeted. While gold prices remained relatively stable, the Economy Ministry of Russia raised vodka prices 40 percent.[7] (See Figure 12.1).

Should the United States ever face similar circumstances, alcohol will surely be a good barter item as citizens try to drink away their problems and numb the new, bleak reality. Lay in your stock of various-sized bottles now—or learn how to set up a backyard still.

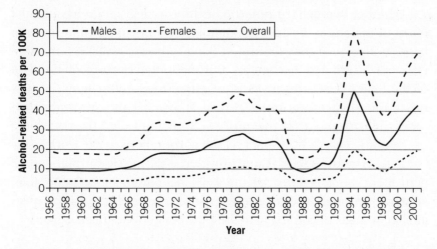

Figure 12.1   One Way to Drown Your Sorrows: Alcohol-Related Deaths in Russia (1956–2002)
Source: *Journal of Drug Issues* 35, no. 1 (2008): 228–247.

And where there's alcohol, can pot be far behind? Pot is portable, has a long shelf life, and can be cultivated indoors or out. Its value as a mind-numbing painkiller is well established and medicinal marijuana is currently legal (at least on a state level) in 16 states.[8]

The Health Care Bomb: Better Have That Surgery Now

The recent health care legislation is already affecting Medicare recipients. The U.S. Department of Health and Human Services' Centers for Medicare and Medicaid Services estimates that the Senate plan takes $493 billion out of Medicare in the next decade. Result: Many doctors and hospitals—most recently the Mayo Clinic—are refusing to participate in the money-losing program, leaving the elderly essentially uninsured.[9]

Government Health Care Exchanges: Already Insolvent

"Whether by intent or not, the health care legislation has had the effect of making it cheaper for many employers to pay fines than to provide insurance for workers—driving uninsured workers into government health-care exchanges. But the long-term projected deficit of the health-care exchanges is an astonishing $38 trillion."

Whether by intent or not, the health care legislation has had the effect of making it cheaper for many employers to pay fines than to provide insurance for workers—driving uninsured workers into government health-care exchanges. But the long-term projected deficit of the health-care exchanges is an astonishing $38 trillion, according to the Medicare Trustees annual report.[10] This is two-and-a-half times the current size of the entire U.S. economy and the equivalent of the market capitalization of all the corporations in the world!

Furthermore, Obamacare provisions will exclude millions of dependent workers who, by the law's definition, have "affordable" employer-provided health insurance for themselves, but "unaffordable" family coverage. According to an Employment Policies Institute study:

> Millions of families will be stuck in a no-man's-land without affordable coverage through their employer or the exchange— because family members of an employee with any offer of coverage are disqualified from accessing subsidized exchange coverage.[11]

And—surprise—under a broad interpretation of "affordable coverage," taxpayers will be stuck with as much as $50 billion more in gross subsidy costs than originally projected. Medicare, Medicaid, and Social Security together represent 40.2 percent of the president's fiscal year 2012 budget—and Medicare spending will triple by 2050 on the current course.[12] (See Figure 12.2.)

Even before health care reform, Medicare's hospital insurance trust fund was set to become insolvent. Obamacare cuts were offered as a way of saving money and extending the life of the program by 12 years. However, Medicare's chief actuary warns that the savings are double-counted and unlikely to materialize, "jeopardizing access to care for beneficiaries."[13] With Medicare going broke and any health care reform fiscally unsound, better have that surgery now if you expect government insurance to pay for it.

Consider a Move to the Country

Should the dollar suffer a precipitous collapse, it may prove easier to survive in the countryside than in the city. In the countryside,

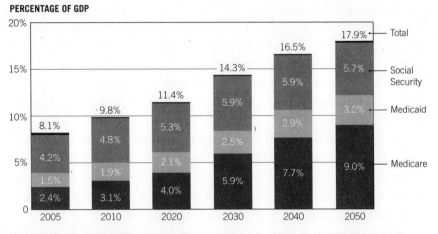

PERCENTAGE OF GDP

Figure 12.2   Runaway Entitlement Spending: Social Security, Medicare, and Medicaid Spending Will Soar as 78 Million Baby Boomers Retire

Source: Congressional Budget Office, The Heritage Foundation.

you can grow your own food, obtain water from your own well, heat your home with locally harvested firewood, and produce electricity with solar and wind power—all insulating you from economic shocks.

Don't wait for a monetary collapse before preparing a move to the country. Why not investigate a rural area where you would like to live? Try a brief stay to get a feel for the community, then rent or buy a vacation property. Experiment with a vegetable patch and learn how to prepare soil and germinate seedlings.

Start acting self-sufficiently now. See what it's like using candles for light or cooking on a barbecue or living without refrigeration. Consider how you will heat your home in the winter, and where you will get fuel to continue running your vehicles.

Above all, get to know your neighbors. In a time of deep economic turmoil, you will learn to rely on one another.

Buy a Generator

When setting up your country retreat, prepare for power outages by buying and installing a generator.

If your goal is to be self-sufficient, start by analyzing your power consumption. Do you need a coffee grinder? A coffee maker? A microwave oven? A washing machine? An electric dryer? Reduce your needs for electricity by substituting manual machinery for power equipment. This can be as simple as opening cans with a hand crank, mowing the lawn with a reel-type mower, or hanging clothes on a line to dry.

More power-saving ideas: Change out incandescent lights with CFLs. Unplug unused gadgets like cell phone chargers. And when buying appliances, look for energy-efficient units that can cut power use long-term and may qualify today for government rebates under the 2009 American Recovery and Reinvestment Act.[14]

Next, determine how many of your appliances will be running at the same time. This will determine your peak power load. At a minimum, you may need to power a well pump, refrigerator, and medical devices like a sleep apnea machine. If you intend to use your generator mainly for power emergencies, a portable generator may be all you need. These are small units that use gasoline as fuel and must be exhausted to the outdoors. Appliances can be plugged in directly. Permanent generators use diesel fuel or propane and are wired to the house with a transfer switch that powers your indoor circuits. Fuel tanks will need to be installed with the generator.

Whether you use a portable or permanent generator, however, it's prudent to run the generator only for a few hours in the morning and evening (to prepare meals, hot water etc.). Running the generator 24/7 wastes fuel that may not be easily replaced.

Go off the Grid

You can take your reduced-energy country lifestyle even further by going off the grid—that is, becoming energy independent from utility-supplied electrical power.

According to *Home Power* magazine, in 2006 there were an estimated 180,000 homes in the United States entirely supplying their own power, and another 27,000 using solar and wind energy to reduce their energy footprint.[15] In most off-grid homes, power is supplied by solar panels (usually mounted on the roof) and/or wind turbines (usually mounted on tall towers). Because sunlight and wind may not be available at exactly the time power is needed, electricity generated by these sources is typically stored in a system of DC batteries and converted to useable AC power by an inverter.

A solar-powered system that provides from 4.5 to 5 kWh for a single-family off-grid home costs around $50,000. This includes solar panels, generators, batteries, inverters, and general fuel and maintenance, and produces energy at a cost of about $0.73 per kilowatt hour.[16] While this is a far cry from the average 20 to 30 kWh consumed by grid-connected consumers, it is adequate for a frugal lifestyle, and the upfront cost is mitigated by avoided costs, like paying to run power lines to the home and, of course, paying for electricity itself.

Homeowners who go off the grid are likely to want to take their lifestyle further and become totally autonomous. This means supplying your own water from a well or cistern and disposing of waste in a septic system. Drilling a well costs from $3,000 to $15,000, and a new septic system runs about $13,000 to $32,000.[17, 18]

How to Avoid Snoopers

If you are worried about government intrusion on your First Amendment privacy, the seizing of tangible assets, or the protection of your identity from snoops and thieves, there are steps you can take to maintain your privacy and keep your assets under the radar.

With the widespread use of computers, your every move can now be traced through routine records. Your telephone company makes a record of every call, the library knows what books you read, deleted files on your computer can be reclaimed, and if you carry a modern cell phone or drive an OnStar equipped vehicle, authorities can trace your location in seconds.

Further, data aggregators like Acxiom, Choicepoint, RapLeaf, Intelius, and Lexis Nexis scour the Internet and various databases to put together surprisingly detailed profiles of your personal information—from Social Security numbers, to phone numbers, to photographs, to favorite websites.[19] Even Visa is getting into the act, selling what it knows about your credit card purchases to Internet advertisers.[20]

Top 10 Opt-Out

Learn the top 10 ways to reduce your exposure to data miners by visiting the World Privacy Forum's website at http://www.worldprivacyforum.org/toptenoptout .html.

Here you will find links to opt out of everything from telemarketer phone calls to intrusive data aggregators—though the process ranges from the simple (a quick phone call) to the Byzantine (letters and snail-mail forms).

But if you are really concerned about protecting your privacy, more extreme measures will be required.

Maintaining Your Privacy in a Facebook World

With the rise of the Internet and continuing exponential leaps in computing power, it has become increasingly difficult for individuals to keep their private lives private. Nonetheless, a careful citizen can take steps to protect assets and make them difficult for snoopers to find.

- Avoid routinely giving out private details like your telephone number, home address, or Social Security number. Use a work, business, or private mailbox street address and create your own variation of the last four digits of your social security number.
- Avoid leaving a credit card trail by paying cash.
- Disperse your Web presence across several providers, using one service for e-mail, another for searches, yet another to access maps, and so on. This will make it harder for any one provider to aggregate details of your personal life and associate them with your Internet I.P. address.
- Stay away from Facebook, MySpace, LinkedIn and other social networking sites that make it easy to learn everything about you. Use private, foreign e-mail address services instead of huge American corporations like Google, Microsoft, or AOL, which are easily hacked. Establish an account with a Virtual Private Network (VPN) and use it routinely, especially

at coffee shops and other wireless hotspots. (VPN traffic is encrypted and requires user authentication.)

- Use your business or LLC to purchase assets and establish a firewall between your business and personal affairs.
- Beware of gadgets like cell phones, webcams, and OnStar, which can be remotely turned into portable bugs, cameras, and/or GPS tracking devices.

These suggestions are only a first line of defense for maintaining your privacy, lowering your profile but not erasing it. They won't deter determined snoopers like skip tracers or maniacal ex-husbands. For that you may need far more elaborate precautions, such as establishing remote or foreign addresses, creating LLCs or corporations that serve as a privacy shield between you and your identity, or laying clues of deliberate misinformation to throw off would-be trackers.

Key Points

- Join with compatriots to hold your representatives' feet to the fire.
- Accounting, plumbing, sewing, farming—develop a skill that will be useful to you and others of your community.
- A weakening dollar makes exporting a good business.
- Learn to protect your privacy from government intrusion.
- Make your vacation home your country refuge.
- Be prepared with food, water, and emergency supplies.
- Power may become erratic in times of severe economic stress.

Conclusion

How to Sleep at Night, Whatever Happens to the Economy

I wouldn't have written this book if I wasn't worried about the ramifications of the U.S. government's massive spending binge and the effect that will have on the value of the dollar and the future of our country. Since the banking bailouts started in 2008, the national debt has exploded from $10 trillion to $15.4 trillion.[1, 2] In 2011, the nation's debt totaled more than 100 percent of the country's GDP.[3] The federal government borrows 43 cents out of every dollar it spends.[4] Millions of Americans are depending on Social Security for their retirement, but the agency will run out of money by 2016, according to the Trustee's own reckoning.[5]

The insanity of the country's finances demands sober leadership and an immediate change of course. No such leadership or change of course is in sight, practically guaranteeing a collision of fiscal promises with fiscal reality. The most likely track for this collision to take is a rapid and accelerating bout of inflation, which will enable the government to meet its obligations by paying for them in devalued currency.

This process is already under way. Food, oil, and other commodities have all been rising in price. The dollar is in an engineered fall against the yuan, the Fed is buying our own long-term bonds, and only chaos in the euro has masked the dollar's growing weakness. Other nations, however, have taken note. Foreign banks are buying huge quantities of gold, and petroleum-producing countries are looking to denominate oil sales in a basket of currencies that deemphasizes the dollar. On top of all these pressures leading to a slow decline in the dollar, war in the Middle East or a sudden spike in the price of oil could cause nervous traders to begin pushing up the price of U.S. bonds, leading to a nightmare hyperinflation scenario like the one that accompanied the death of the Soviet Union.

However, as individuals, there is a limit to how much any one of us will be able to do to correct the folly of our leaders. Awaiting the government inflation debacle is a little like awaiting a hurricane— you know a big storm is coming, but you're powerless to stop it and you're not sure what the damage level will be.

Whatever happens to the economy, the one way you'll be able to sleep at night is to take action now. Move at least a portion of your wealth into anti-inflation investments: to commodities like oil, timber, and precious metals; to foreign currencies, businesses, and bonds; or to real estate purchased with fixed-rate mortgages. Have a plan in case the infrastructure goes down or begins operating erratically. Have cash on hand for bank closures or ATM failures, and coins and barter items in case the dollar destabilizes rapidly. Develop useful hobbies like gardening or medical skills and fix up that retirement home in the country. (Who knows—you may want to retire early.) Try these and other strategies suggested throughout this book.

No one knows when—or how violently—inflation will kick up. But you can rest easier knowing you took prudent steps to protect your family's wealth while you had time.

Then let come what may.

Notes

Preface

1. Kerri Shannon, "Federal Budget Deficit Climbing Dangerously Higher on Continued 2011 Government Spending," *MoneyMorning.com*, January 27, 2012, http://moneymorning.com/2011/01/27/federal-budget-deficit-climbing-dangerously-higher-on-continued-2011-government-spending/ (accessed April 3, 2012).
2. Jacob Goldstein, "$13 Trillion: The Projected 10-Year Deficit," *NPR.org*, July 14, 2011, http://www.npr.org/blogs/money/2011/07/15/137845220/-13-trillion-the-projected-10-year-deficit (accessed November 11, 2011).
3. Mark Knoller, "National Debt Has Increased $4 Trillion under Obama," *CBSNews.com*, August 22, 2011, http://www.cbsnews.com/8301-503544_162-20095704-503544.html (accessed November 11, 2011).
4. Zeke Miller, "National Debt Increased Under Obama Faster Than Any Other President," *Businessinsider.com*, August 23, 2011, http://articles.businessinsider.com/2011-08-23/politics/30018770_1_national-debt-bush-tax-cuts-president-barack-obama (accessed November 11, 2011).
5. Lori Montgomery, "National Debt to Be Higher than White House Forecast, CBO Says," *Washingtonpost.com*, March 6, 2010, http://www.washingtonpost.com/wp-dyn/content/article/2010/03/05/AR2010030502974.html (accessed November 11, 2011).
6. Brian Riedl, "Obama Budget Adds $80,000 per Household to National Debt," *The Foundry*, March 23, 2011, http://blog.heritage.org/2011/03/23/obama-budget-adds-80000-per-household-to-national-debt/ (accessed November 25, 2011).
7. Dennis Cauchon, "Government's Mountain of Debt," *USATODAY.com*, June 7, 2011, http://www.usatoday.com/news/washington/2011-06-06-us-debt-chart-medicare-social-security_n.htm (accessed November 25, 2011).

Chapter 1

1. Jeff Cox, "US Is in Even Worse Shape Financially Than Greece: Gross," *CNBC*, June 13, 2011, http://www.cnbc.com/id/43378973/US_Is_in_Even_Worse_Shape_Financially_Than_Greece_Gross (accessed February 3, 2012).

2. Bruce Bartlett, "How Excessive Government Killed Ancient Rome," *The Cato Journal*, Fall 1994, http://www.cato.org/pubs/journal/cjv14n2-7.html (accessed November 15, 2011).

3. Brendan Conway, "Dow Up 135.63; Gold Recedes," *Wall Street Journal*, December 30, 2011, http://online.wsj.com/article/SB1000142405297020472 02045771281505141685842.html (accessed December 31, 2011).

4. Glenn Hubburt, "It's Still Possible to Cut Spending: Here's How," *Wall Street Journal*, November 23, 2011, http://online.wsj.com/article/SB1000142405297 02045314045770521701666023222.html.

5. *Red Ink Rising: A Call to Action to Stem the Mounting Federal Debt*. Report. Petersen-Pew Commission on Budget Reform, 2009. Print.

6. "Inflation, List by Country," *Trading Economics*, http://www.tradingeconomics .com (accessed November 15, 2011).

7. George J. W. Goodman, *Paper Money*, New York: Summit, 1981. Quoted in: "Commanding Heights: The German Hyperinflation, 1923," *PBS: Public Broadcasting Service*, November 15, 2011, http://www.pbs.org/wgbh/commanding heights/shared/minitext/ess_germanhyperinflation.html.

8. Steve H. Hanke, "Zimbabwe Inflation." *Individual Liberty, Free Markets, and Peace*, The Cato Institute, November 15, 2011, http://www.cato.org/ zimbabwe.

9. Patrick McGroarty and Farai Mutsaka, "Zimbabwe's 100-Trillion-Dollar Bill Is a Hot Collectible," *Wall Street Journal*, May 11, 2011, http://online.wsj.com/article/ SB10001424052748703730804576314953091790360.html (accessed November 15, 2011).

10. "Memorial Day Cookout Will Cost You 29% More This Year Thanks to Inflation," *Mail Online*, May 26, 2011, http://www.dailymail.co.uk/news/ article-1390822/Memorial-Day-cookout-cost-29-year-thanks-inflation.html (accessed November 15, 2011).

11. Jeff Wilson, "Thanksgiving Meal Cost Jumps 13% as Turkey Fuels Food Inflation," *Bloomberg Businessweek*, November 14, 2011, http://www.businessweek .com/news/2011-11-14/thanksgiving-meal-cost-jumps-13-as-turkey-fuels-food-inflation.html (accessed November 15, 2011).

12. Julie Schmit and Barbara Hansen, "Rising Rents Make Housing Less Affordable," *USATODAY.com*, September 22, 2011, http://www.usatoday .com/money/economy/housing/story/2011-09-22/housing-affordability/ 50499656/1 (accessed November 15, 2011).

13. Justin T. Hilley, "Freddie Mac: Rental Housing Rises in 2011," *HousingWire*, October 17, 2011, http://www.housingwire.com/2011/10/17/freddie-mac-rental-housing-rising-in-2011 (accessed November 15, 2011).

14. "Despite Price Drop for Cotton, Shoppers Unlikely to Get Break," *ToledoBlade.com*, October 30, 2011, http://www.toledoblade.com/Retail/2011/10/30/Despite-price-drop-for-cotton-shoppers-unlikely-to-get-break.html (accessed November 15, 2011).

15. Annalyn Censky, "Gas, Food and Clothing Prices Are on the Rise," *CNNMoney*, August 18, 2011, http://money.cnn.com/2011/08/18/news/economy/inflation_cpi/ (accessed November 15, 2011).

16. Gary Strauss, "Higher Gas Prices Pinch Consumers," *USATODAY.com*, May 20, 2011, http://www.usatoday.com/money/industries/energy/2011-05-19-gas-prices-poll_n.htm (accessed November 16, 2011).

17. Ronald D. White, "Gas Prices Might Be Headed to Record Highs in 2012, Analysts Say," *Los Angeles Times*, November 8, 2011, http://articles.latimes.com/2011/nov/08/business/la-fi-gas-prices-20111108 (accessed November 16, 2011).

18. Reed Abelson, "Health Insurance Costs Rising Sharply This Year, Study Shows," *New York Times*, September 27, 2011, http://www.nytimes.com/2011/09/28/business/health-insurance-costs-rise-sharply-this-year-study-shows.html?pagewanted=all (accessed November 16, 2011).

19. Nancy-Ann DeParle, "Health Insurance Premium Update," *The White House Blog*, September 27, 2011, http://www.whitehouse.gov/blog/2011/09/27/health-insurance-premium-update (accessed November 16, 2011).

20. Steven K. Beckner, "St. Louis Fed Study Says QE Devalued Dollar by 6.5 to 11 Percent," *Gold Anti-Trust Action Committee*, June 30, 2011, http://gata.org/node/10067 (accessed November 16, 2011).

Chapter 2

1. Housing prices from http://www.thepeoplehistory.com.

2. "Uses of Gold in Industry, Medicine, Computers, Electronics, Jewelry," *Geology.com*, http://geology.com/minerals/gold/uses-of-gold.shtml (accessed November 16, 2011).

3. Ibid.

4. Rhiannon Hoyle, "Central Banks Continue to Buy Gold," *Wall Street Journal*, September 29, 2011, http://online.wsj.com/article/SB10001424052972020422 6204576598940803518426.html (accessed November 16, 2011).

5. "Gold Set to Continue Gaining Value Next Year, Another Financial Firm Predicts," *Daniels Trading*, October 7, 2011, http://www.danielstrading.com (accessed November 16, 2011).

6. "Gold Up 26% in 2011," Fox Business Video, *Fox News*, November 10, 2011, http://video.foxbusiness.com/v/1268512643001/ (accessed November 16, 2011).

7. Thomas Kutty Abraham and Kim Kyoungwha, "India Buys IMF Gold to Boost Reserves as Dollar Drops (Update2)." *Bloomberg Business & Financial News*, November 3, 2009, http://www.bloomberg.com/apps/news?pid=newsarchive&sid=aa6oc6Wz9Ftg (accessed November 16, 2011).

8. Francesco Guerrera, "A Golden Age for Gold Has Lost Some of Its Luster," *Wall Street Journal*, October 4, 2011.

9. Sergey Kadinsky, "Should You Buy Gold Now?" *CBSNews.com*, June 8, 2010, http://www.cbsnews.com/2100-504343_162-5953150.html (accessed November 19, 2011).

10. Shane Heffernan, "Why Buy Gold and Copper?" *Commodities & Futures, International Business Times*, October 1, 2011, http://www.google.com/url?q=http://www.ibtimes.com/articles/223250/20111001/why-buy-gold-and-copper.htm&sa=U&ei=TX58T_22AcnVtgeb9NmRDQ&ved=0CAQQFjAA&client=internal-uds-cse&usg=AFQjCNEtqVJlzQkq8b315gyrfAEySJR3IA. (accessed November 19, 2011).

11. Rhiannon Hoyle, "Central Banks in Scramble to Buy Gold," *WSJ Blogs*, November 17, 2011, http://blogs.wsj.com/marketbeat/2011/11/17/central-banks-in-scramble-to-buy-gold/.

12. Frik Els, "China Tops Indian Gold Jewelry Demand for First Time," *Mining.com*, November 17, 2011, http://www.mining.com/2011/11/17/china-tops-indian-gold-jewelry-demand-for-first-time/.

13. "USA "GLD"—Frequently Asked Questions—SPDR Gold Shares," *Spdrgoldshares.com*, November 25, 2011, http://www.spdrgoldshares.com/sites/us/faqs/.

14. Brad Zigler, "How Much Gold Should Be in Your Portfolio?" *Mineweb*, June 2, 2009, http://www.mineweb.com/mineweb/view/mineweb/en/page33?oid=84224&sn=Detail (accessed November 19, 2011).

15. "Demand and Supply," *World Gold Council*, November 21, 2011, http://www.gold.org/investment/why_how_and_where/why_invest/demand_and_supply/.

16. Brian Reed, "High Gold Prices: Factors That Made Gold This Decade's Best Investment," *InvestingAnswers.com*, October 20, 2011, http://www.investinganswers.com/investment-ideas/commodities-precious-metals/4-factors-made-gold-decades-best-investment-3754.

17. "Gold Up 26% in 2011," *Fox News*, November 10, 2011, http://video.foxbusiness.com/v/1268512643001/gold-up-26-in-2011/.

18. Mike Obel, "Gold Rebounds With Other Safe Havens," *IBTimes Gold, Ibtimes.com*, September 16, 2011, http://www.ibtimes.com/articles/215043/20110916/gold-silver-euro-dollar-banks-central-federal-reserve.htm.

19. "Gold and Economic Uncertainty," Message to the author, November 23, 2011, www.InvestmentArtsCorp.com.

20. Jan Harvey and Frank Tang, "Gold to Clear $2,000 in 2012 as Rally Cools: LBMA Poll," Reuters India, in.reuters.com, September 20, 2011, http://in.reuters.com/article/2011/09/20/us-gold-lbma-idINTRE78J5S320110920.

21. Glenys Sim, "'Resilient' Gold May Surge to Record as Economy Slows, Morgan Stanley Says," *Bloomberg*, October 7, 2011, http://www.bloomberg.com/news/2011-10-07/-resilient-gold-may-rally-to-record-as-economy-slows-morgan-stanley-says.html.

22. "Gold Could Top US$2,500 an Ounce and Might Even Hit US$5,000, Says Citigroup," *Proactiveinvestors UK*, July 29, 2011, http://www.proactiveinvestors.co.uk/companies/news/31307/gold-could-top-us2500-an-ounce-and-might-even-hit-us5000-says-citigroup-31307.html (accessed February 20, 2012).

23. Melissa Pistilli, "Could The Price of Gold Reach Past $2,500 in 2012?" *Gold Investing News*, September 20, 2011, http://goldinvestingnews.com/17909/could-the-price-of-gold-reach-past-2500-in-2012.html.

24. Laurence Hunt, "Gold's 1980 High—Think $5000—No $8000—per Ounce—or Higher," *Laurence Hunt's Blog*, February 15, 2011, http://laurencehunt.blogspot.com/2007/07/golds-1980-high-think-5000-per-ounce.html.

25. "Snapshot of the Amt. of Dollars in Circulation per One Oz. of Gold," Fisher Precious Metals, November 29, 2010, http://fisherpreciousmetals.com/2010/11/53957-in-circulation-for-every-ounce-of-gold/ (accessed December 19, 2011).

26. Jan Harvey and Frank Tang, "Gold to Clear $2,000 in 2012 as Rally Cools: LBMA Poll," Reuters India, in.reuters.com, September 20, 2011, http://in.reuters.com/article/2011/09/20/us-gold-lbma-idINTRE78J5S320110920.

27. Ibid.

28. Gus Lubin, "Roubini: Gold Is in a Hyperbolic Bubble," *Business Insider*, August 23, 2011, http://www.businessinsider.com/roubini-gold-is-in-a-bubble-2011-8.

29. "Reserves," *Government Affairs*, World Gold Council, November 25, 2011, http://www.gold.org/government_affairs/gold_reserves/.

30. Eleanor Laise, "Risks Lurk for ETF Investors," *Wall Street Journal*, February 1, 2010.

31. "Right to Financial Privacy Act," *Access Reports, Freedom of Information Act and Privacy Issues*, February 6, 2012, http://www.accessreports.com/statutes/RFPA.htm.

32. "Protecting Financial Privacy: The Burden Is on You," Privacy Rights Clearinghouse, April 2010, http://www.privacyrights.org/fs/fs24-finpriv.htm (accessed February 6, 2012).

33. Fred von Lohmann, "Subpoenas and Your Privacy," Electronic Frontier Foundation, February 4, 2006, https://www.eff.org/deeplinks/2006/02/subpoenas-and-your-privacy (accessed February 6, 2012).

34. Casey Smith, "ETFs vs. ETNs; You Better Be Careful," *wiserinvestor.com*, March 3, 2009, http://www.wiserinvestor.com/etfs-vs-etns-you-better-be-careful/ (accessed February 6, 2012).

35. Ben Protess, "MF Global Trustee Says Shortfall Could Exceed $1.2 Billion," *New York Times*, November 21, 2011, http://dealbook.nytimes.com/2011/11/21/mf-global-trustee-estimates-shortfall-could-be-more-than-1-2-billion/ (accessed February 5, 2012).

36. Paul Joseph Watson, "MF Global Looted Customers' Accounts via Internal Bank Run," *Alex Jones' Infowars*, November 16, 2011, http://www.infowars.com/mf-global-looted-customers-accounts-via-internal-bank-run/.

37. Robert Higgs, "How FDR Made the Depression Worse," *The Free Market*, Ludwig Von Mises Institute, February 1995, http://mises.org/freemarket_detail.aspx?control=258 (accessed November 25, 2011).

38. Dorothy Kosich, "President Chavez Signs Decree Nationalizing Venezuelan Gold Mining Sector," *Mineweb*, August 24, 2011, http://www.mineweb.com/mineweb/view/mineweb/en/page72068?oid=134062&sn=Detail (accessed November 25, 2011).

39. Michael Lombardi, "The Gold-to-Silver Ratio: Why It's Important, What It's Telling Us Today," *Wall Street Pit*, August 5, 2011, http://www.google.com/url?q=http://wallstreetpit.com/80937-the-gold-to-silver-ratio-why-its-important-what-its-telling-us-today&sa=U&ei=04J8T6qbN-j50gHNt9n5Cw&ved=0CAQQFjAA&client=internal-uds-cse&usg=AFQjCNEJ4lHpXZnq0mlf2MZ6NNHqnxlZ7A.

40. Jason Hommel, "Silver vs. Gold," *Gold-Eagle.com*, August 1, 2004, http://www.gold-eagle.com/editorials_04/hommel080104.html (accessed November 25, 2011).

41. "George Maniere: Silver Beaten Down by Strong Dollar," *BabyBullTwits*, November 25, 2011, http://babybulltwits.wordpress.com/category/silver/page/4/.

42. Golden Economizer, "12 Reasons Why Silver Will Outperform Gold," *Seeking Alpha*, April 17, 2011, http://seekingalpha.com/article/263874-12-reasons-why-silver-will-outperform-gold (accessed November 25, 2011).

43. "Overview—IShares Silver Trust," *IShares Exchange Traded Funds*, November 25, 2011, http://us.ishares.com/product_info/fund/overview/SLV.htm.

Chapter 3

1. Jack Hough, "Finally, Time to Buy a House," *Online Investing: Stocks, Personal Finance & Mutual Funds at SmartMoney.com*, November 1, 2011, http://www.smartmoney.com/spend/real-estate/finally-time-to-buy-a-house-1318604163856.

2. "Dallas, TX Real Estate, Apartments & Houses for Rent," *HotPads—Map Search for Real Estate, Apartments and Houses for Rent, Foreclosures and Homes for Sale*, November 3, 2011, http://hotpads.com/search/city/TX/Dallas.

3. Nick Timiraos, "Rising Rents Surpass Mortgage Payments," *Wall Street Journal*, November 26–27, 2011.

4. "Should You Rent or Buy?" *SmartMoney.com*, February 28, 2011, http://www.smartmoney.com/spend/real-estate/to-rent-or-to-buy-9687/

5. Joe Arsenault, "Passive and Nonpassive Business Rules," *CafeTax Personal Finance & Tax*, February 7, 2011 http://www.cafetax.com/2011/02/07/passive-and-nonpassive-business-rules/.

6. Bill Bischoff, "So You Want to Be a Landlord," *SmartMoney.com*, May 16, 2008, http://www.smartmoney.com/taxes/income/so-you-want-to-be-a-landlord-17987/ (accessed November 28, 2011).

7. Diane Kennedy, "Are You a Real Estate Professional? Maybe Not, Says IRS," *Realty Times*, July 17, 2008, http://realtytimes.com/rtpages/20080717_realpro.htm (accessed November 28, 2011).

8. Lee Egerstrom, "Home Equity Protection Plan Tried, Worked in Syracuse," *MN2020*, May 7, 2009, http://www.mn2020.org/issues-that-matter/economic-developmentfiscal-policy/home-equity-protection-plan-tried-worked-in-syracuse (accessed November 28, 2011).

9. Lisa Scherzer, "Should You Buy a Home Equity Protection Plan?" *SmartMoney.com*, May 26, 2011, http://www.smartmoney.com/spend/real-estate/should-you-buy-a-home-equity-protection-plan/.

10. Lee Egerstrom, "Stopping the Freefall: Stabilizing Minnesota's Housing Market," *MN2020*, March 15, 2009, http://www.mn2020.org/issues-that-matter/economic-development/stopping-the-freefall-stabilizing-minnesota-s-housing-market (accessed November 28, 2011).

11. Joshua Cohn, "When Looking at Agriculture, Don't Overlook Direct Investment In Farmland," *Seeking Alpha*, October 24, 2011, http://seekingalpha.com/article/301670-when-looking-at-agriculture-don-t-overlook-direct-investment-in-farmland.

12. Callan Associates, "Farmland Investing: An Overview," December 2005, http://www.callan.com/research/download/?file=papers%2Ffree%2F47.pdf (accessed November 7, 2011).

13. Mark Peters and Scott Kilman, "A Bubble Down on the Farm?" *Wall Street Journal*, December 15, 2011, http://online.wsj.com/article/SB10001424052970204844504577098581283225666.html.

14. Gonzalo Lira, "SPG Supplement: Is Farmland a Smart Hedge against Inflation?" *Gonzalo Lira* (blog), May 25, 2011, http://gonzalolira.blogspot.com/2011/05/spg-supplement-is-farmland-smart-hedge.html.

Chapter 4

1. Chris Kahn, "Crude Oil Hits $100, First Time since July," *USATODAY.com*, November 16, 2011, http://www.usatoday.com/money/economy/inflation/story/2011-11-16/Oil-prices-hit-100/51234160/1.

2. Robert Fisk, "Oil Not Priced in Dollars by 2018?" *Bloomberg Businessweek*, October 6, 2009, http://www.businessweek.com/globalbiz/content/oct2009/gb2009106_736291.htm (accessed December 2, 2011).

3. John Vidal, "WikiLeaks Cables: Saudi Arabia Cannot Pump Enough Oil to Keep a Lid on Prices," *The Guardian*, February 8, 2011, http://www.guardian.co.uk/business/2011/feb/08/saudi-oil-reserves-overstated-wikileaks.

4. Adam Grubb, "Peak Oil Primer," *Energy Bulletin*, Post Carbon Institute, October 20, 2011, http://www.energybulletin.net/primer.php.

5. Report on the Risks and Impacts of a Potential Future Decline in Oil Production. Rep. no. 11D/707. Washington: Department of Energy & Climate Change, June 1, 2009, http://www.decc.gov.uk/assets/decc/What%20we%20do/Global%20climate%20change%20and%20energy/International%20energy/energy%20security/1790-decc-report-2009-oil-decline.pptx.

6. Lawrence C. Strauss, "Whatever Happens in Egypt, Oil Will Hit $300 by 2020," *Barron's Online*, February 12, 2011, http://online.barrons.com/article/SB50001424052970204098404576130370708044708.html (accessed December 2, 2011).

7. "Abiotic Theory," The Environmental Literacy Council, April 2, 2008, http://www.enviroliteracy.org/article.php/1130.html (accessed December 2, 2011).

8. Daniel Yergin, "There Will Be Oil," *Wsj.com*, September 17, 2011, http://online.wsj.com/article/SB10001424053111904060604576572552998674340.html.

9. Susan Lyon, Rebecca Lefton, and Daniel J. Weiss, "Quenching Our Thirst for Oil," Center for American Progress, April 23, 2010, http://www.americanprogress .org/issues/2010/04/oil_quench.html (accessed December 2, 2011).

10. Larry Elliott, "Oil Price May Hit $150, Warns International Energy Agency," *The Guardian*, November 9, 2011, http://www.guardian.co.uk/business/2011/ nov/09/international-energy-agency-oil-price.

11. Jeff McMahon, "Those New Gulf Oil-Drilling Permits? Not So New," *Forbes.com*, March 25, 2011, http://www.forbes.com/sites/jeffmcmahon/2011/03/25/ those-new-gulf-oil-drilling-permits-not-so-new/ (accessed December 6, 2011).

12. Paul M. Barrett, "Could Shale Gas Reignite the U.S. Economy?" *Bloomberg Businessweek*, November 3, 2011, http://www.businessweek.com/magazine/ could-shale-gas-reignite-the-us-economy-11032011.html.

13. David Lee Smith, "Fracking Should Benefit From Shareholders' Attention." *Fool .com (The Motley Fool)*, June 3, 2011, http://www.fool.com/investing/general/ 2011/06/03/fracking-should-benefit-from-shareholders-attentio.aspx (accessed December 6, 2011).

14. Ibid.

15. Keith Kohl, *Shale Shock: How to Invest in Hydraulic Fracturing* (Rep. Energy and Capital: Angel Publishing LLC, May 2011).

16. Barbara Balfour, "The Income Trusts 'Halloween Massacre': Handling the Fallout One Year on" *The Lawyers Weekly*, September 14, 2007, http://www.lawyersweekly .ca/index.php?section=article&articleid=538 (accessed December 6, 2011).

17. "Canadian Income Securities," *The Yield Hunter*, December 6, 2011, http://www .dividendyieldhunter.com/Canadian_Oil_and_Gas_Trusts_Master_List.html.

Chapter 5

1. Anna Prior, "Investing in Gold? Try Platinum," *Smart Money*, September 26, 2011, http://www.smartmoney.com/invest/strategies/investing-in-gold-try-platinum- 1315930971070/.

2. John Stepek, "This Precious Metal Hasn't Been so Cheap in 20 Years," *MoneyWeek*, November 8, 2011, http://www.moneyweek.com/investments/ precious-metals-and-gems/other/investing-in-platinum-14500.

3. "About the Precious Metal Platinum," *Silvertrading.net*, December 6, 2011, http://www.silvertrading.net/platinum_aboutplatinum.html.

4. Michelle Madsen, "Russia's Palladium Stockpiles Impossible to Estimate," *CommodityOnline*, November 23, 2010, http://www.google.com/url?q=http:// www.commodityonline.com/news/russias-palladium-stockpiles-impossible-to- estimate-33678-3-33679.html&sa=U&ei=wG2ET7HCD8nWtgfSt62GCA&ved =0CAUQFjAA&client=internal-uds-cse&usg=AFQjCNH6xf0uQstfwKknEwsV bTYrnvJFJA (accessed December 7, 2011.

5. Mike Obel, "Russia's Palladium Stockpile to Be Gone in Two Years," *IBTimes .com*, December 1, 2011, http://www.ibtimes.com/articles/259728/20111201/ russia-s-palladium-stockpile-gone-years.htm.

6. Elroy Dimson and Christophe Spaenjers, "Ex Post: The Investment Performance of Collectible Stamps," *Journal of Financial Economics* 100, no. 2 (2011). Available at SSRN: http://ssrn.com/abstract=1444341.

7. Jack Shamash, "Stamps Do Not Always Deliver Top Investment Returns," *The Guardian*, August 6, 2010, http://www.guardian.co.uk/money/2010/aug/07/stamps-gibbons-harmers-investment.

8. "De Beers and Alrosa Break Ties and Making Room for Competition," *Diamond Price Guide, Jewelry Store News*, July 5, 2010, http://www.diamondpriceguide.com/news/nc208_Most-Popular/n87875_De-Beers-and-Alrosa-Break-Ties-and-Making-Room-for-Competition.

9. "Competition: De Beers' Commitment to Phase Out Rough Diamond Purchases from ALROSA," *Europa Press Releases RAPID*, February 22, 2006, http://europa.eu/rapid/pressReleasesAction.do?reference=MEMO/06/90&format=HTML&aged=0&language=EN&guiLanguage=en (accessed December 27, 2011).

10. Melissa Pistilli, "India and China Boosting 2011 Diamond Market," *Diamond Investing News*, May 11, 2011, http://diamondinvestingnews.com/3007-india-and-china-boosting-2011-diamond-market.html.

11. Geraldine Fabrikant, "The King of Really Big Diamonds Heads to China," *New York Times*, June 18, 2011, http://www.nytimes.com/2011/06/19/business/global/19jewels.html?pagewanted=all.

12. Dusan Stojanovic, "The Gemstone Forecaster," *Preciousgemstones.com*, Winter 2009, http://www.preciousgemstones.com/gfwinter09.html.

13. Marhy Pilon, "Is Art the Next Boom Investment?" *Wall Street Journal*, May 22, 2010, http://online.wsj.com/article/SB10001424052748704513104575256783908983328.html.

14. Ibid.

15. Jianping Mei and Michael Moses, "The Investment and Asset Potential of Art," *Beautiful Asset Advisors, The Mei Moses Fine Art Index*, December 12, 2011.

16. Richard Friswell, "Art Economist Michael Moses Looks Objectively at Wealth Management for Art Collectors, with Historically-Based Auction Analysis," *Artes Magazine*, May 3, 2011, http://www.artesmagazine.com/2011/05/art-economist-michael-moses-looks-objectively-at-wealth-management-for-art-collectors-with-historically-based-auction-analysis/.

17. Larry D. Spears, "Timber Investing: The Inflation Hedge That Pays Off in Every Type of Market," *Moneymorning.com*, February 25, 2011, http://moneymorning.com/2011/02/25/timber-investing-inflation-hedge-pays-off-every-type-market/.

18. Tony D'Altorio, "Investing in Timber," *InvestmentU.com*, December 12, 2011, http://www.google.ca/url?sa=t&rct=j&q=&source=web&cd=1&ved=0CDwQFjAA&url=http%3A%2F%2Fwww.investmentu.com%2Fresearch%2Ftimber-investing.html&ei=ynCET_frBZDWiAKR88z6BA&usg=AFQjCNF8vLQRrlyvhcZNldgBov716Q0Nkw&cad=rja.

19. Larry D. Spears, "Timber Investing: The Inflation Hedge That Pays Off in Every Type of Market," *Moneymorning.com*, February 25, 2011, http://moneymorning.com/2011/02/25/timber-investing-inflation-hedge-pays-off-every-type-market/.

20. "Investment Guru Small Cap Stock Observer," *InvestmentGuru.com*. March 23, 2011, http://www.investorsguru.com/homepage.html%3bjsessionid=0EEAF6 650B099D84374C87D174D4E257.

21. Dexter Dombro, "What Have Others Said about Investing in Timber?" *Co2tropicaltrees.blogspot.com, Investing in Tropical Trees*, September 23, 2009, http://co2tropicaltrees.blogspot.com/2009/09/what-have-others-said-about-investing.html.

22. "Timberland Investments in an Institutional Portfolio," Copenhagen: International Woodland, March 11, 2011, http://www.iwc.dk/publications/2_ Tbld%20investments%20in%20an%20institutional%20portfolio.pdf.

23. "A Timely and Intelligent Investment," *Ecologixrg.com*, Ecologix Resource Group, Inc., 2010, accessed December 12, 2011.

24. Paul Strurm, "Timber!" *Panamateakforestry.com*, December 12, 2011, http:// www.google.ca/url?sa=t&rct=j&q=&source=web&cd=1&ved=0CCoQFjAA& url=http%3A%2F%2Fwww.panamateakforestry.com%2Fenglish%2 Finvestments_teak%2Farticles%2Fsmartmoneybuystimber.php&ei=9XGET_fxI avYiQK3iPj1BA&usg=AFQjCNFbOmx0Su94GhcyoNwtX6KEnYuvFw&cad=rja.

25. Paul V. Ellefson and Michael A. Kilgore, "United States Wood-Based Industry: A Review of Structure and Organization," Staff Paper Series Number 206, January 2010, http://conservancy.umn.edu/bitstream/107774/1/206.pdf .

26. "Investing in Timber," *Timber Investment Report, Whiskey and Gunpowder*, December 12, 2011, http://whiskeyandgunpowder.com/free-reports/ timber-investment-report/.

27. Eric Pryne, "REIT Generated Growth for Plum Creek," *Seattle Times*, August 3, 2008, http://seattletimes.nwsource.com/html/businesstechnology/2008088337_ reit03.html.

28. "Food Costs Will Increase 4% in 2011, USDA Says in Raising its Projection." February 24, 2011. http://articles.latimes.com/2011/feb/24/business/ la-fi-food-prices-20110224.

29. "Surge in Food Inflation Hits Both Consumers and Retailers, WSJ.com, October 26, 2011, http://online.wsj.com/article/SB100014240529702046445 04576653120117664898.html.

30. "What's Driving Food Prices in 2011?" *Farm Foundation*, July 19, 2011, http:// www.farmfoundation.org/webcontent/Whats-Driving-Food-Prices-in-2011- 1742.aspx?z=85&a=1742.

31. Jason White, "9 Ways to Prepare for Food Inflation," *FrugalDad.com*, January 18, 2011, http://frugaldad.com/2011/01/18/prepare-for-food-inflation.

32. "Belarus Threatened with 70% Annual Inflation Rate," *Belsat TV*, August 18, 2011, http://belsat.eu/en/wiadomosci/a,4405,belarus-threatened-with-70- annual-inflation-rate.html.

33. Aliaksandr Kudrytski, "Belarus Runs Out of Meat as Russians Exploit Currency Plunge," *Bloomberg Businessweek*, August 31, 2011, http://www.bloomberg .com/news/2011-08-30/belarus-runs-out-of-meat-amid-currency-plunge.html.

34. Jae Hur and Ichiro Suzuki, "Copper May Have Shortage for Third Year on China Demand, Pan Pacific Says," *Bloomberg*, September 4, 2011, http://www.bloomberg.com/news/2011-09-05/copper-may-have-shortage-for-third-year-on-china-demand-pan-pacific-says.html.

35. "Copper Theft: The Growing Epidemic," *Coppertheft.info*. RSI Video Technologies, December 12, 2011, http://coppertheft.info/.

36. Michael Johnston, "Copper ETFs in Focus: 5 Ways To Play Metal," *Seeking Alpha*, December 5, 2011, http://seekingalpha.com/article/311963-copper-etfs-in-focus-5-ways-to-play-metal.

Chapter 6

1. J. D. Roth, "Mortgage Prepayment Made Easy: Own Your Home in Half the Time," *Get Rich Slowly*, February 12, 2008, http://www.getrichslowly.org/blog/2008/02/12/mortgage-prepayment-made-easy-own-your-home-in-half-the-time.

2. Quoted in J. D. Roth, "Ask the Readers: Is It Better to Invest or to Prepay a Mortgage?" *Get Rich Slowly*, June 1, 2007, http://www.getrichslowly.org/blog/2007/06/01/ask-the-readers-is-it-better-to-invest-or-to-prepay-a-mortgage.

3. "CoreLogic Reports 24 Percent Decrease in Foreclosures," *RISMedia*, February 21, 2012, http://rismedia.com/2012-02-09/corelogic%C2%AE-reports-24-percent-decrease-in-foreclosures.

4. Diana Olick, "Foreclosures on the Rise Again," *CNBC.com*, February 16, 2012, http://www.cnbc.com/id/46401756/Foreclosures_on_the_Rise_Again.

5. "Home Loan Modifications on the Rise," *Loan Modification Leads*, May 9, 2011, http://www.loanmodificationleads.com/blog.

6. Arthur Delaney, "Homeowners Protest HAMP: 'It's Just a Scam and the Banks Are Getting Everything'," *Huffington Post*, October 26, 2010, http://www.huffingtonpost.com/2010/10/26/homeowners-protest-hamp-i_n_773582.html.

7. Steve Beede, "National Mortgage Settlement—A Win for Banks—More Hype for Homeowners," *SteveBeede.com*, February 9, 2012, http://stevebeede.com/tag/loan-modification.

8. "How to Negotiate with Your Mortgage Lender," *Interest.com*, May 20, 2011, http://www.interest.com/debt/news/how-to-negotiate-with-your-mortgage-lender/.

9. "Delay Tactics," *PreventingForeclosure.org*, February 21, 2012, http://preventingforeclosure.org/stop-a-foreclosure/delay-tactics/.

10. Elizabeth Weintraub, "Should You Choose a Short Sale over a Foreclosure?" *About.com*, February 21, 2012, http://homebuying.about.com/od/foreclosures/f/072509_Short-Sale-vs-Foreclosure.htm.

11. Gary North, "Skip Toll-Free," *Gary North's Tip of the Week* (February 11, 2012), e-mail.

12. "FDIC Law, Regulations, Related Acts," *FDIC: Federal Deposit Insurance Corporation*, November 9, 1987, http://www.fdic.gov/regulations/laws/rules/4000-2660.html (accessed December 29, 2011).

13. "8 Charts from a Brave New Banking and Economic System," *My Budget 360 Blog*, December 29, 2011, http://www.mybudget360.com/brave-new-banking-and-economic-system-federal-reserve-banking-jobs-money-fdic-low-wage-growth.

14. Jonathan Weil, "FDIC Is Broke, Taxpayers at Risk, Bair Muses," *Bloomberg*, September 23, 2009, http://www.bloomberg.com/apps/news?pid=newsarchive&sid=aEKc7Yh8ogXw.

15. John Woolley and Gerhard Peters, "Franklin D. Roosevelt: Proclamation 2039—Declaring Bank Holiday," *The American Presidency Project*, December 29, 2011, http://www.presidency.ucsb.edu/ws/index.php?pid=14661.

16. Drea Knufken, "25 Biggest Bank Failures in History," *Business Pundit*, May 7, 2009, http://www.businesspundit.com/25-biggest-bank-failures-in-history/.

17. "Failed Bank List," *FDIC: Federal Deposit Insurance Corporation*, December 20, 2011, http://www.fdic.gov/bank/individual/failed/banklist.html.

18. At least a few larger depositors lost money at failed banks in 2010 because their deposits exceeded FDIC insurance. See "FDIC Warns Banks on Potential Losses by Depositors," *Problem Bank List*, February 8, 2011, http://problembanklist.com/fdic-warns-banks-on-potential-losses-by-depositors-0307/.

19. Erin E. Arvedlund, "The Silver Rush at MF Global," *Barron's*, December 17, 2011, http://online.barrons.com/article/SB5000142405274870385680457709874032263760.html.

20. John Carney, "Citigroup Warns Customers It May Refuse to Allow Withdrawals," *The Business Insider*, February 19, 2010, http://articles.businessinsider.com/2010-02-19/wall_street/30047096_1_fdic-coverage-7-day-notice-accounts.

21. Chris Isidore, "Obama Wants Cheaper Pennies and Nickels," *CNNMoney*, February 15, 2012, http://money.cnn.com/2012/02/15/news/economy/pennies_nickels/.

22. "Composition of US Coins," *Composition and Reedings of US Coins*, February 21, 2012, http://www.fleur-de-coin.com/coinfacts/unitedstates_1.asp.

23. "1965 Coin Act Changes the Face of U.S. Coins," *The Fun Times Guide to U.S. Coins*, February 21, 2012, http://coins.thefuntimesguide.com/2009/03/1965_coins.php.

24. "Current Melt Value of Coins—How Much Is Your Coin Worth?" *Current Melt Value of Coins*, February 21, 2012, http://www.coinflation.com.

Chapter 7

1. Cf., "Credit Card Pitfalls," *Consumer Reports*, May 2008, http://www.consumerreports.org/cro/aboutus/mission/viewpoint/credit-card-pitfalls-5-08/overview/credit-card-rates-ov.htm (accessed January 30, 2012).

2. The White House, *Fact Sheet: Reforms to Protect American Credit Card Holders*, *Whitehouse.gov*, May 22, 2009, http://www.whitehouse.gov/the_press_office/Fact-Sheet-Reforms-to-Protect-American-Credit-Card-Holders.

3. Jessica Silver-Greenberg, "The New Credit-Card Tricks," *Wall Street Journal,* July 31, 2010, http://online.wsj.com/article/SB10001424052748704895004575395 823497473064.html.

4. Reed Allmand, "Debtor Beware: More Dirty Credit Card Tricks," *Allmand Law,* August 9, 2010, http://www.google.ca/url?sa=t&rct=j&q=&source=web& cd=2&ved=0CC8QFjAB&url=http%3A%2F%2Fallmandlaw.com%2Fcredit-counseling%2Fdebtor-beware-more-dirty-credit-card-tricks&ei=WEuIT8isB4if twfckPjFCQ&usg=AFQjCNHNHXdq-tIoUWZhloaAhMN5xmfwOA&cad=rja.

5. "Gold Reserve Act of 1934 Definition," *Investopedia.com,* December 13, 2011, http://www.investopedia.com/terms/g/gold-reserve-act-1934.asp.

6. "A Golden Rent," *New York Sun,* September 3, 2008, http://www.nysun.com/editorials/a-golden-rent/85086/.

7. "Postponing Repayment," *Student Aid on the Web,* Federal Student Aid, May 31, 2011, http://studentaid.ed.gov/PORTALSWebApp/students/english/difficulty .jsp.

8. "4 Requirements for Student Loan Forbearance," *Loan.com,* December 13, 2011, http://www.loan.com/student-loans/number-requirements-for-student-loan-forbearance.html.

9. Stephen C. Fehr, "Tracking the Recession: Tuition Programs in Danger," *Stateline.org,* Pew Center on the States, April 20, 2009, http://www.stateline .org/live/details/story?contentId=393552.

10. Ron Lieber, "College Plans You Thought Were Safe," *New York Times,* April 1, 2011, http://www.nytimes.com.

11. Steve Daniels and Paul Merrion, "Crain's Investigation: Illinois' Prepaid Tuition Plan Struggles as College Costs Soar," *www.chicagobusiness.com,* March 7, 2011, http://www.chicagobusiness.com/article/20110305/ISSUE01/303059975/ crains-investigation-illinois-prepaid-tuition-plan-struggles-as-college-costs-soar.

12. Ron Lieber, "College Plans You Thought Were Safe," *New York Times,* April 1, 2011, http://www.nytimes.com/2011/04/02/your-money/paying-for-college/02money .html.

Chapter 8

1. "Bretton Woods Agreement," *Investopedia.com,* December 14, 2011, http:// www.investopedia.com/terms/b/brettonwoodsagreement.asp.

2. Roger Lowenstein, "The Nixon Shock," *Bloomberg Businessweek,* August 4, 2011, http://www.businessweek.com/magazine/the-nixon-shock-08042011.html.

3. "Budget Explorer: The Complete U.S. Federal Budget," *Kowal Design,* December 14, 2011, http://www.kowaldesign.com/budget/.

4. Ralph Benko, "Fiat Money: The Root Cause of Our Financial Disaster," *Forbes .com,* August 15, 2011, http://www.forbes.com/sites/ralphbenko/2011/08/15/ fiat-money-the-root-cause-of-our-financial-disaster/.

5. Barry Eichengreen, "Dollar's Reign as World's Main Reserve Currency Is Near an End," *Wall Street Journal*, March 2, 2011, http://online.wsj.com/article/SB1 0001424052748703313304576132170181013248.html.

6. Shayne Heffernan, "Why Buy Gold and Copper?" *IBTimes.com*, October 1, 2011, http://www.google.ca/url?sa=t&rct=j&q=&source=web&cd=1&ved= 0CC4QFjAA&url=http%3A%2F%2Fwww.ibtimes.com%2Farticles%2F223250 %2F20111001%2Fwhy-buy-gold-and-copper.htm&ei=7kyIT9v1OM2ltwfCnZG zCQ&usg=AFQjCNH8xDWaVCv8ivuLMvFN5h5JGxcwDQ&cad=rja.

7. Brian Sullivan, "Brian Sullivan: Currencies, Gold and Euro Bailout," *CNBC*, December 1, 2011, http://www.cnbc.com/id/45390716/Brian_ Sullivan_Currencies_Gold_and_Euro_Bailout.

8. "U.S. Dollar Outlook: 2012 Greenback Strength vs Euro, Yen, Aussie and Loonie," *Savingtoinvest.com*, December 14, 2011, http://www.savingtoinvest .com/2008/05/us-dollar-outlook-2008-2009-and-beyond.html.

9. Simon Evenett, "What Happens If U.S. Interest Rates Continue to Rise?" *Dr. Evenett's Blog, The St. Gallen MBA*, January 14, 2011, http://stgallenmba.ch/ evenett/2011/01/14/what-happens-if-us-interest-rates-continue-to-rise/.

10. Barry Eichengreen, "Dollar's Reign as World's Main Reserve Currency Is Near an End," *Wall Street Journal*, March 2, 2011, http://online.wsj.com/article/SB1 0001424052748703313304576132170181013248.html.

11. Craig K. Elwell, *Dollar Crisis: Prospect and Implications, CRS Report for Congress*, Rep. no. RL34311. Washington: Congressional Research Service, January 8, 2008.

12. "Foreign Currencies Backed by Gold," forexonlinelearning.com, 2012, http://www.forexonlinelearning.com/foreign-currencies-backed-by-gold/.

13. "Future Outlook of the Chinese Yuan," *World Currency Information, Currency Information and Research*, November 8, 2011, http://currencyinformation.org/ Future-of-the-Chinese-Yuan.htm.

14. Brian Bremner, Chester Dawson, Assif Shameen, and Moon Ihlwan, "The Yuan Grows Up," *Bloomberg Businessweek*, August 8, 2005, http://www.businessweek .com/magazine/content/05_32/b3946147_mz035.htm.

15. Philip Aldrick, "U.S. and Britain Avert 'Currency War' by Securing Agreement with China to Let Yuan Rise in Value," *Telegraph.co.uk*, November 8, 2011, http://www.telegraph.co.uk/finance/china-business/8870677/US-and-Britain-avert-currency-war-by-securing-agreement-with-China-to-let-yuan-rise-in-value.html.

16. "Congress and the China Currency Bill," *Leeb's Market Forecast*, October 17, 2011, http://www.leeb.com/long-term-growth/congress-and-china-currency-bill-10-17-11.

17. Tom Barclay and Sudeep Reddy, "U.S. Won't Cite China on Yuan's Slow Rise," *Wall Street Journal*, December 28, 2011, http://online.wsj.com/article/SB2000 1424052970203479104577124962748590078.html.

18. Joshus Klein Lipman, "Law of Yuan Price: Estimating Equilibrium of the Renminbi," *Michigan Journal of Business* 4, no. 2 (2011).

19. Charles Wallace, "Here's a New Way to Bet on China: Open a Renminbi Bank Account," *Dailyfinance.com*, January 14, 2011, http://www.dailyfinance .com/2011/01/14/china-currency-renminbi-bank-account/.

20. Zach Honig, "I Have a Chinese Bank Account–And Why You Should Too!" *Tech, Travel & Tuna Blog*, January 21, 2011, http://techtravelandtuna .com/2011/01/21/i-have-a-chinese-bank-account-and-why-you-should-too/.

21. Alena Mikhan and Andrey Dashkov, "Renminbi Kilobar–Another Sign of China's Growing Role in the Gold Market," *Casey Research, Casey's Daily Dispatch*, October 20, 2011, http://www.caseyresearch.com/cdd/invest-gold-and-chinese-renminbi.

22. "Hong Kong Becomes First Centre for Gold Trading in Yuan," *BBC*, October 16, 2011, http://www.bbc.co.uk/news/business-15330664.

23. Jonathan Standing, "Fitch Warns of Downgrades for China, Japan," *Financial Post*, September 8, 2011, http://www.reuters.com/article/2011/09/08/ us-fitch-idUSTRE7870WI20110908.

24. Belinda Cao and Michael Patterson, "Chinese Banks' Bad Debt May Hit 60% of Equity Capital, Credit Suisse Says," *Bloomberg*, October 12, 2011, http:// www.bloomberg.com/news/2011-10-12/chinese-banks-bad-debt-may-hit-60-of- equity-capital-credit-suisse-says.html.

25. "Even China Accuses China of Fibbing about Inflation," Weblog post. *Fund My Mutual Fund*, November 12, 2010, http://www.fundmymutualfund .com/2010/11/even-china-accuses-china-of-fibbing.html.

26. Patricia S. Pollard, "The Creation of the Euro and the Role of the Dollar in International Markets," *Federal Reserve Bank of St. Louis*. Rep. Sept/Oct 2001.

27. Sabine Kurjo McNeill, "The Problems with the Euro," *Forum for Stable Currencies, Monday Club*, January 8, 2012, http://forumforstablecurrencies .info/category/money-supply/.

28. "List of European Union Countries," *EU Country List*, January 8, 2012, http:// www.eucountrylist.com.

29. Markus Walker, Charles Forelle, and Stacy Meichtry, "Deepening Crisis Over Euro Pits Leader Against Leader," *Wall Street Journal*, December 30, 2011, http://online .wsj.com/article/SB10001424052970203391104577124480046463576.html.

30. Lindsay Amantea, "The Problem with the Euro," *Politonomist.com*, July 7, 2011, http://www.politonomist.com/the-problem-with-the-euro-002647/.

31. Martin Wolf, "Merkozy Failed to Save the Eurozone," *Financial Times*, December 6, 2011, http://www.ft.com/cms/s/0/396ff020-1ffd-11e1-8662- 00144feabdc0.html.

32. Derek DeCloet, "The Solution to Europe's Problems? Sell Assets," *The Globe and Mail*, December 30, 2011, http://www.theglobeandmail.com/report- on-business/rob-magazine/the-solution-to-europes-problems-sell-assets/ article2282449.

33. David Oakley, "Greek Bond Yields Rise to Unprecedented Levels," *Financial Times*, September 13, 2011, http://www.ft.com/cms/s/0/afd72cac-de07-11e0- a115-00144feabdc0.html.

34. Tom Fairless, "Latest Greek Bailout Called Insufficient; Report," *Marketwatch .com*, *Wall Street Journal*, January 6, 2012, http://www.marketwatch.com/story/latest-greek-bailout-called-insufficient-report-2012-01-06.

35. "The World Factbook," *Central Intelligence Agency*, 2010, https://www.cia.gov/library/publications/the-world-factbook/rankorder/2186rank.html.

36. Markus Walker, Charles Forelle, and Stacy Meichtry, "Deepening Crisis Over Euro Pits Leader Against Leader," *Wall Street Journal*, December 30, 2011, http://online.wsj.com/article/SB10001424052970203391104577124480046463576.html.

37. "The World Factbook," *Central Intelligence Agency*, 2010, https://www.cia.gov/library/publications/the-world-factbook/rankorder/2186rank.html.

38. Moritz Kraemer, and Frank Gill, "Standard & Poor's Puts Ratings on Eurozone Sovereigns on CreditWatch with Negative Implications," *Standard & Poor's*, December 5, 2011, http://www.standardandpoors.com/fgr_article/en/us?object_id=7011613&rev_id=1.

39. Markus Walker, Charles Forelle, and Stacy Meichtry, "Deepening Crisis Over Euro Pits Leader Against Leader," *Wall Street Journal*, December 30, 2011, http://online.wsj.com/article/SB10001424052970203391104577124480046463576.html.

40. Imogen Lloyd Webber, "Euro Collapse and the American Impact," *Huffington Post*, January 6, 2012, http://www.huffingtonpost.com/imogen-lloyd-webber/euro-collapse-and-the-ame_b_1189254.html.

41. Paul Krugman, "Killing the Euro" *New York Times*, December 1, 2011, http://www.nytimes.com/2011/12/02/opinion/krugman-killing-the-euro.html.

42. Dakin Campbell, "U.S. Banks Face Contagion Risk from Europe Debt," *Bloomberg*, November 17, 2011, http://www.bloomberg.com/news/2011-11-16/banks-in-u-s-facing-serious-risk-on-contagion-from-europe-fitch-says.html.

43. "Monthly Exchange Rate Average (American Dollar, Canadian Dollar) 2009," *Exchange Rates*, *X-rates.com*, December 19, 2011, http://www.x-rates.com/d/USD/CAD/hist2009.html.

44. "World Bond Top Performers: Mutual Funds Center," *Top News Archive*, Yahoo! *Finance*, December 19, 2011.

45. "European Public Debt at a Glance," accessed October 28, 2011, http://edition.cnn.com/2011/BUSINESS/06/19/europe.debt.explainer/index.html.

46. Abigail Moses, "Greece Has 98% Chance of Default on Euro-Region Sovereign Woes," *Bloomberg*, September 13, 2011, http://www.bloomberg.com/news/2011-09-12/greece-s-risk-of-default-increases-to-98-as-european-debt-crisis-deepens.html.

47. *Global Sovereign Credit Risk Report*, Rep. CMA, March 30, 2010, http://www.cmavision.com/images/uploads/docs/CMA_Global_Sovereign_Credit_Risk_Report_Q1_2010.pdf.

48. Gregory Zuckerman, "Buying Bonds of Low-Debt Nations and How to Bet Against the Dollar," *Wall Street Journal*, June 14, 2010.

49. Ron Rowland, "Norway Gets Single Country ETF," *Seeking Alpha*, November 12, 2010, http://seekingalpha.com/article/236478-norway-gets-single-country-etf.

50. Louis Basenese, "Investing in South Korea," *Investment U*, August 26, 2010, http://www.investmentu.com/2010/August/investing-in-south-korea.html.

51. "Quarterly Inventory Report on All Metal Bars," *Quarterly Vault Inventory Reports*, *GoldMoney*, September 30, 2011, http://www.goldmoney.com/vault-reports.html.

52. "Rates and Fees for Buying, Selling, Storing and Exchanging Precious Metals," *GoldMoney*, December 19, 2011, http://www.goldmoney.com/fees.html.

53. "In Depth—Gold Bars Held in Storage," *Pecunix*, July 2011, http://pecunix .com/money.refined...ind.goldbars.

54. "Federal Grand Jury Indicts E-Gold," *World Law Direct*, April 27, 2007, http:// www.worldlawdirect.com/article/3268/federal-grand-jury-indicts-e-gold.html.

55. Douglas Jackson, "E-gold Value Access Plan—Monetization Preparation," *E-gold Blog*, August 12, 2011, http://blog.e-gold.com/.

56. "A Complete Guide to Agriculture ETFs," *Seeking Alpha*, June 24, 2009, http:// seekingalpha.com/article/145094-a-complete-guide-to-agriculture-etfs.

Chapter 9

1. "Daily Treasury Yield Curve Rates," *U.S. Department of the Treasury*, December 15, 2011, http://www.treasury.gov/resource-center/data-chart-center/interest-rates/ Pages/TextView.aspx?data=yield.

2. "2011 Commentary," *Oppenheimer Commodity Strategy Total Return Fund*, September 30, 2011, https://www.oppenheimerfunds.com/digitalAssets/ Commodity-Strategy-Total-0571598f-31ce-4055-9775-52e463e9952b.pd.

3. "The Decrease in Purchasing Power of the U.S. Dollar since 1900," *Observations*, May 13, 2011, http://observationsandnotes.blogspot.com/2011/04/100-year-declining-value-of-us-dollar.html.

4. "Obama Predicts 'Trillion-Dollar Deficits for Years to Come,'" *Fox News*, January 6, 2009, http://www.foxnews.com/politics/2009/01/06/obama-predicts-trillion-dollar-deficits-years-come/

5. Antal E. Fekete, "Has Hedging Killed the Goose That Was to Lay the Golden Egg?" *Safehaven.com*, September 15, 2008, http://www.safehaven.com/ article/11247/has-hedging-killed-the-goose-that-was-to-lay-the-golden-egg.

6. Jacob Goldstein, "Fed's 'Operation Twist,' Explained In 4 Easy Steps," *Planet Money*, *NPR*, September 21, 2011, http://www.npr.org/blogs/ money/2011/09/21/140643696/operation-twist-explained-in-4-easy-steps.

7. Dave Carpenter, "What Fed's 'Operation Twist' Means for You," *USA Today*, September 22, 2011, http://www.usatoday.com/money/economy/ story/2011-09-22/Fed-Consumer/50511514/1.

8. Eric Parnell, "Operation Twist Leaves the Market Wrung Out," *Seeking Alpha*, November 17, 2011, http://seekingalpha.com/article/308766-operation-twist-leaves-the-market-wrung-out.

9. "U.S. Federal Reserve Continues 'Operation Twist' Stimulus," *BBC News*, December 13, 2011, http://www.bbc.co.uk/news/business-16171138.

10. Daniel Indiviglio, "The Fed's Twist May Increase Inequality," *Atlantic*, September 26, 2011, http://www.theatlantic.com/business/archive/2011/09/the-feds-twist-may-increase-inequality/245672/.

11. "TIPS In Depth," *TreasuryDirect.gov*, U.S. Department of the Treasury, May 11, 2011, http://www.treasurydirect.gov/indiv/research/indepth/tips/res_tips.htm.

12. "Frequently Asked Questions," *Consumer Price Index*, U.S. Bureau of Labor Statistics, October 19, 2011, http://www.bls.gov/cpi/cpifaq.htm.

13. Barbara Hagenbaugh, "Food, Energy Costs' Exclusion Debated," *USA Today*, June 14, 2007, http://www.usatoday.com/money/economy/inflation/2007-06-13-inflation-usat_N.htm.

14. J. Roger Shealy, *Consumer Price Index (CPI)—If You Can't Win the Game, Change the Rules*, Rep. SKadvisors, LLC, April 27, 2006, http://www.skadvisors.com/CPI.pdf.

15. Quoted in: J. Roger Shealy, *Consumer Price Index (CPI)—If You Can't Win the Game, Change the Rules*, Rep. SKadvisors, LLC, April 27, 2006, http://www.skadvisors.com/CPI.pdf.

16. "Self-Directed 401(k) Accounts and 401(k) Plans," *Self Directed IRA and Roth 401(k) Accounts for Real Estate Business and Tax Lien Investors*, December 16, 2011, http://www.selfdirectediraaccounts.com/401k.html

17. Dan Caplinger, "Why You Need a Self-Directed IRA," *Fool.com*. The Motley Fool, January 8, 2009, http://www.fool.com/investing/ira/2009/01/08/why-you-need-a-self-directed-ira.aspx.

18. "Blaze Your Own IRA Trail," *Bloomberg Businessweek*, February 6, 2006, http://www.businessweek.com/magazine/content/06_06/b3970114.htm.

19. Anna Maria Andriotis, "5 Reasons to Convert to a Roth IRA," *Smart Money*, September 15, 2009, http://www.smartmoney.com/retirement/planning/5-reasons-to-convert-to-a-roth-ira/.

20. Annie Gasparro, "Why You Shouldn't Convert to a Roth IRA," *Wall Street Journal*, June 14, 2010, http://online.wsj.com/article/SB10001424052748703315404575250141315548882.html.

21. Robert S. Keebler, "Five Reasons Not To Convert To a Roth IRA," *Forbes.com*, March 10, 2010, http://www.forbes.com/2010/03/09/roth-ira-conversion-tax-retirement-personal-finance-5-reasons-not-convert.html.

Chapter 10

1. "Total U.S. Labor Force vs. Total U.S. Government Workers," *WolframAlpha*, December 22, 2011, http://www.wolframalpha.com/input/?i=total+US+labor+force+vs.+total+US+government+workers.

2. Christopher Chantrill, "U.S. Federal Debt by Year," *Government Spending in United States: Federal State Local for 2011*, usgovernmentspending.com, December 22, 2011.

3. Elmer T. Peterson, "This Is the Hard Core of Freedom," *Daily Oklahoman* [Oklahoma City], December 9, 1951.

4. Jeanne Sahadi, "Bush Tax Cuts: The Real Endgame," *CNNMoney*, November 28, 2011, http://money.cnn.com/2011/11/28/news/economy/bush_tax_cuts/.

5. Chuck Raasch, "Bush Tax Cuts Complicate Efforts on Debt," *USA Today*, November 30, 2011, http://www.usatoday.com/news/washington/story/2011-11-30/bush-tax-cuts-debt-debate/51509084/1.

6. Tino Sanandaji, "The Bush Tax Cuts Lower Revenue by 1.7% of GDP," *Super-Economy*, August 9, 2011, http://super-economy.blogspot.com/2011/08/bush-tax-cuts-lower-revenue-by-15-of.html.

7. "Tax Statistics," *Internal Revenue Service*, July 27, 2011, http://www.irs.gov/taxstats/index.html.

8. "Transcript: Obama's State of the Union Address," *NPR*, January 25, 2011, http://www.npr.org/2011/01/26/133224933/transcript-obamas-state-of-union-address.

9. Richard Wolf and Gregory Korte, "State of the Union: Fact-checking Obama's Speech," *USA Today*, January 26, 2011, http://www.usatoday.com/news/washington/2011-01-25-state-of-the-union-fact-check_N.htm.

10. "Office of Management and Budget," *The White House*, December 28, 2011, http://www.whitehouse.gov/omb.

11. Jeanne Sahadi, "Proposed Deficit Fixes Still Miss the Big Picture," *CNNMoney*, January 25, 2011, http://money.cnn.com/2011/01/25/news/economy/deficit_proposals/.

12. "Who Said Socialism Works until You Run out of Other People's Money," *The Q&A Wiki*, answers.com, January 8, 2012, http://wiki.answers.com/Q/Who_said_socialism_works_until_you_run_out_of_other_people%27s_money.

13. Qiu Huafei and Huang Ye," "The Dilemma of Rational Choice: A Case on EMU and Sovereign Debt Crisis," Working paper no. SIES-WP-VOL2011-No3, Shanghai: Shanghai Institute for European Studies, March 2011.

14. "Onze Questions-reponses Sur La Crise Grecque." *Le Nouvel Observateur*, May 5, 2010, http://tempsreel.nouvelobs.com/economie/20100505.OBS3509/onze-questions-reponses-sur-la-crise-grecque.html.

15. Ibid.

16. Henry Blodget, "Greece Paid Goldman $300 Million to Help It Hide Its Ballooning Debts," *Business Insider*, February 14, 2010, http://articles.business insider.com/2010-02-14/wall_street/30065714_1_greece-goldman-sachs-currency-trade.

17. "Greece's Sovereign-debt Crunch: A Very European Crisis," *Economist* February 4, 2010.

18. "Greek Protesters Hurl Stones, Gas Bombs," *MSNBC*, October 19, 2011, http://www.msnbc.msn.com/id/44955899/ns/world_news-europe/t/weve-lost-everything-violent-day-strike-shuts-down-greece/.

19. Stephen Fidler, Matthew Dalton, and Alkman Granitsas, "Greece Sets Austerity Plan," *Wall Street Journal*, February 10, 2012, http://online.wsj.com/article/SB10001424052970203646004577212293337077400.html.

20. "Greenspan: Greek Default Likely as Europe 'Very Dangerous,'" *moneynews.com*, October 7, 2011, http://www.moneynews.com/Headline/Greenspan-Greek-Default-Europe/2011/10/07/id/413619.
21. Kimberly Amadeo, "U.S. Federal Debt and Deficit—How the National Debt and Deficit Are Different and How the Debt and Deficit Affect Each Other," *About.com*, January 10, 2011, http://useconomy.about.com/od/fiscalpolicy/p/US_Debt_Deficit.htm.
22. Brian Faier and Julianna Goldman, "U.S. Deficit for 2009 Totals $1.4 Trillion, Budget Office Says," *Bloomberg*, October 8, 2009, http://www.bloomberg.com/apps/news?pid=newsarchive&sid=aA8lChe4zUQU.
23. David Jackson, "Obama on Deficit and Debt Critics: 'I'm Calling Their Bluff,'" *USA Today*, June 28, 2010, http://content.usatoday.com/communities/theoval/post/2010/06/obama-signals-coming-battle-over-debt/1.
24. Congressional Budget Office, *The Long-Term Budget Outlook*, Rep. no. Doc10297 (Washington: Congressional Budget Office, June 2009).
25. Eleanor Clift, "Grover Norquist: Don't Give an Inch on Taxes!" *Daily Beast*, December 1, 2011, http://www.thedailybeast.com/articles/2011/11/30/grover-norquist-don-t-give-an-inch-on-taxes.html.
26. Robert Reich, "Republicans Will Tax Anyone but the Rich," *Christian Science Monitor*, December 6, 2011, http://www.csmonitor.com/Business/Robert-Reich/2011/1206/Republicans-will-tax-anyone-but-the-rich.
27. Bonnie Goodman, "How Did the Present Alternative Minimum Tax Come into Existence?" *History News Network*, June 20, 2005, http://hnn.us/articles/11819.html.
28. "EP Abusive Tax Transactions—Deductions for Excess Life Insurance in a Section 412(i) or Other Defined Benefit Plan," *Internal Revenue Service*, January 14, 2011, http://www.irs.gov/retirement/article/0,,id=120449,00.html.
29. Huma Khan, "Obama's Budget: Almost $1 Trillion in New Taxes Over Next 10 Yrs, Starting 2011," *Political Punch, ABC News*, February 26, 2009, http://abcnews.go.com/blogs/politics/2009/02/obamas-budget-a/.
30. "A Reckless Health Care Bill That Nobody Believes In," *Wall Street Journal*, December 21, 2009, http://online.wsj.com/article/SB10001424052748704398304574598130440164954.html.
31. *The Federal Government's Long-Term Fiscal Outlook*. Rep. no. GAO-11-451SP, Updated ed. (Washington D.C.: United States Government Accountability Office, 2011).
32. Peter Orszag, "One Nation, Two Deficits," *The Opinion Pages, New York Times*, September 6, 2010, http://www.nytimes.com/2010/09/07/opinion/07orszag.html?pagewanted=all.
33. Joseph Rago and Paul A. Gigot, "On Taxes, 'Modeling,' and the Vision Thing," *The Weekend Interview with Mitt Romney, Wall Street Journal*, December 24, 2011, http://online.wsj.com/article/SB100014240529702044644045771145917844220950.html.

34. PricewaterhouseCoopers LLP, "Tax Policy in a Deficit-driving World: 2011 Tax Legislative Outlook," (Washington: Washington National Tax Services, January 2011), http://www.pwc.com/en_US/us/washington-national-tax/ assets/tax-policy-deficit-driven-world-tax-leg-outlook.pdf.

35. "Les Recettes Fiscales," *Le Forum de la Performance*, Ministere du Budget des Comptes Publics et de la Reforme de L'etat, December 28, 2011, http:// www.performance-publique.budget.gouv.fr/le-budget-et-les-comptes-de-letat/ approfondir/les-recettes/les-recettes-fiscales.html.

36. "Europe's VAT Lessons," *online.wsj.com*, April 15, 2011, http://online.wsj .com/article/SB10001424052702304198004575172190620528592.html.

37. Alan S. Blinder, "Keynesian Economics," *The Concise Encyclopedia of Economics*, October 30, 2011, http://www.econlib.org/library/Enc1/KeynesianEconomics .html.

38. Mark Thorton, "Austrian Recipe vs. Keynesian Fantasy," *Mises.org*, Ludwig Von Mises Institute, May 21, 2009, http://mises.org/daily/3465.

39. Conn Carroll, "True Cost of Stimulus: $3.27 Trillion," *Heritage.org*, The Heritage Foundation, February 12, 2009, http://blog.heritage.org/2009/02/ 12/true-cost-of-stimulus-327-trillion/.

40. Bob Willis and Carol Massar, "Krugman Says U.S. Should Do 'Everything We Can' to Boost Jobs," *Bloomberg.com*, *July 6, 2010*, http://www.bloomberg.com/ news/2010-07-06/krugman-says-kitchen-sink-strategy-needed-to-stave-off-another-recession.html.

41. Allan H. Meltzer, "Four Reasons Keynesians Keep Getting it Wrong," *Wall Street Journal*, Oct. 28, 2011, http://online.wsj.com/article/SB1000142405297 02047779045766515327212 67002.html.

42. Mark Thorton, "Austrian Recipe vs. Keynesian Fantasy," *Mises.org*, Ludwig Von Mises Institute, May 21, 2009, http://mises.org/daily/3465.

43. Michael Snyder, "22 Statistics That Prove the Middle Class Is Being Systematically Wiped Out of Existence in America," *Business Insider*, July 14, 2010, http://www.businessinsider.com/22-statistics-that-prove-the-middle-class-is-being-systematically-wiped-out-of-existence-in-america-2010-7.

44. Mark J. Perry, "Personal Bankruptcy Filings Decline 11.6% in 2011," *Carpe Diem*, January 12, 2012, http://mjperry.blogspot.com/2012/01/personal-bankruptcy-filings-decline-by.html.

45. Mark Gongloff and Lila Shapiro, "Jobs Report: As Many As Three Million Long-Term Unemployed Not Counted As Jobless Rate Drops," *Huffington Post*, February 3, 2012, http://www.huffingtonpost.com/2012/02/03/us-economy-adds-tktk-jobs_n_1252209.html.

46. Jon Gertner, "Does America Need Manufacturing?" *New York Times*, August 24, 2011, http://www.nytimes.com/2011/08/28/magazine/does-america-need-manufacturing.html?pagewanted=all.

47. "Foreign Trade: Data," *Census Bureau Homepage*, February 10, 2012, http:// www.census.gov/foreign-trade/data/.

48. Jon Gertner, "Does America Need Manufacturing?" *New York Times*, August 24, 2011, http://www.nytimes.com/2011/08/28/magazine/does-america-need-manufacturing.html?pagewanted=all.

49. Patrick J. Buchanan, "A Decade of Self-Delusion," *Humanevents.com*, December 29, 2009, http://www.humanevents.com/article.php?id=35018.

50. David Ignatius, "A Bleak Look at America's Future," *Washington Post*, December 9, 2011, http://www.washingtonpost.com/opinions/a-bleak-look-at-americas-future/2011/12/09/gIQAAYmDjO_story.html.

Chapter 11

1. Richard D. Anderson, *Monetary Base*, Rep. no. 2006-049A (St. Louis, MO: Federal Reserve Bank of St. Louis, Research Division, August 2006), http://research.stlouisfed.org/wp/2006/2006-049.pdf.

2. "Financial Reporting in Hyperinflationary Economies," International Accounting Standard No. 29 (IAS 29), http://www.worldgaapinfo.com/pdf/IAS/IAS29.pdf.

3. Allan H. Meltzer, "The Fed's Anti-inflation Exit Strategy Will Fail," *American Enterprise Institute for Public Policy Research*, January 28, 2010, http://www.aei.org/article/economics/monetary-policy/the-feds-anti-inflation-exit-strategy-will-fail/.

4. Tim Ahmann, "Bernanke Says Strong Dollar in U.S. and Global Interest," Reuters, April 27, 2011, http://www.reuters.com/article/2011/04/27/us-usa-fed-dollar-idUSTRE73Q7BH20110427.

5. "Obama, China President Hu Share Intimate White House Dinner," *Fox News*, January 19, 2011, http://www.foxnews.com/politics/2011/01/18/large-docket-table-china-presidents-visit/.

6. Jeb Handwerger, "Why the U.S. and China Secretly Want a Devalued U.S. Dollar," *IStockAnalyst*, May 9, 2011, http://www.istockanalyst.com/finance/story/5128378/why-the-u-s-and-china-secretly-want-a-devalued-u-s-dollar.

7. "Fed Extends Dollar Swap Lines with Central Banks," Reuters, June 29, 2011, http://www.reuters.com/article/2011/06/29/usa-fed-ecb-swap-idUSN1E75S0FH20110629.

8. Mike Norman, "Fed Extends Dollar Swap Lines to Foreign Central Banks–AGAIN!" *Mike Norman Economics*, June 29, 2011, http://mikenormaneconomics.blogspot.com/2011/06/fed-extends-dollar-swap-lines-to.html.

9. Liam Halligan, "Benign Neglect May Turn the Dollar from a Safe Haven to a Dangerous Place to Be," *Telegraph*, November 28, 2009, http://www.telegraph.co.uk/finance/economics/6678334/Benign-neglect-may-turn-the-dollar-from-a-safe-haven-to-a-dangerous-place-to-be.html.

10. Anthony C. LoBaido, "Land-grab Policy Causes Zimbabwe Famine," *A Free Press for A Free People*, WorldNetDaily, November 20, 2001, http://www.wnd.com/2001/11/11725/.

11. Steve H. Hanke, "Zimbabwe Inflation," *The Cato Institute*, May 3, 2010, http://www.cato.org/zimbabwe.

12. Mike Nizza, "Zimbabwe Confident after Losing Cash Machine," *The Lede Blog, New York Times,* July 3, 2008, http://thelede.blogs.nytimes.com/2008/07/03/zimbabwe-confident-after-losing-cash-machine/.

13. Alan Greenspan, "U.S. Debt and the Greece Analogy," *Wall Street Journal,* June 18, 2010, http://online.wsj.com/article/SB10001424052748704198004575310962247772540.html.

14. "Survive Hyperinflation—Common Sense Ideas and Suggestions (Update #2)," *Larry Myles Reports,* December 31, 2011, http://www.larrymylesreports.com/Survive_Hyperinflation.htm.

15. "What Is the Banking Act of 1933?" *WiseGEEK,* December 29, 2011, http://www.wisegeek.com/what-is-the-banking-act-of-1933.htm.

16. "Multinational Corporations, 1955–1990*,"* *Encyclopedia of the New American Nation,* December 29, 2011, http://www.americanforeignrelations.com/E-N/Multinational-Corporations-Multinational-corporations-1955-1990.html.

17. Chris Mack, "Silver Spikes and Power Struggles," *Seeking Alpha,* August 7, 2010, http://seekingalpha.com/article/219358-silver-spikes-and-power-struggles.

18. "Franklin D. Roosevelt: Executive Order 8734 Establishing the Office of Price Administration and Civilian Supply," *The American Presidency Project,* December 30, 2011, http://www.presidency.ucsb.edu/ws/index.php?pid=16099.

19. "Nixon Imposes Wage and Price Controls," *The Econ Review,* December 30, 2011, http://www.econreview.com/events/wageprice1971b.htm.

20. Art Carden, "The Unintended Consequences of Rent Control," *Ludwig Von Mises Institute,* August 5, 2009, http://mises.org/daily/3483.

21. B A R K I, "Russia: How Do They Survive?" 1998 (est.), http://econ.la.psu.edu/~bickes/survival.pdf.

22. Eric Kraus, "The Missing Chapter–A Personal View of Russia Twenty Years After," *Truth & Beauty [. . . And Russian Finance],* October 14, 2011, http://www.truthandbeauty.ru/featured-item/the-missing-chapter-%E2%80%93-a-personal-view-of-russia%E2%80%93twenty-years-after.

Chapter 12

1. Floyd Norris, "As U.S. Exports Soar, It's Not All Soybeans," *New York Times,* February 11, 2011, http://www.nytimes.com/2011/02/12/business/economy/12charts.html.

2. Lauren Keiper, "13 Dead, Millions without Power after Rare U.S. Storm," *Reuters.com,* November 1, 2011, http://www.reuters.com/article/2011/11/01/uk-usa-weather-idUSLNE7A002V20111101.

3. Olivia Katrandjian and Colleen Curry, "Hurricane Irene: 8 Dead, 2 Million Without Power—ABC News," *ABCNews.com,* August 27, 2011, http://abcnews.go.com/US/hurricanes/hurricane-irene-dead-million-power/story?id=14393026.

4. Yegor Gaidar, "The Soviet Collapse," *AEI,* April 2007, http://www.aei.org/issue/25991.

5. Branko Milanovic, *Income, Inequality, and Poverty during the Transformation from Planned to Market Economy* (Washington DC: The World Bank, 1998), 186–90.

6. William Alex Pridemore, "Patterns of Alcohol-Related Mortality in Russia," *Journal of Drug Issues* 36, 1 (2006): 229–247, http://www.ncbi.nlm.nih.gov/pmc/articles/PMC1534076.

7. Steven Leckart, "Apocalypse 101," *Wired* Magazine, July 2011, http://www.wired.com/magazine/2010/06/pl_ask_algorithm/.

8. "16 Legal Medical Marijuana States and DC—Medical Marijuana," *Procon.org*, October 25, 2011, http://medicalmarijuana.procon.org/view.resource.php?resourceID=000881.

9. Conn Carroll, "Obamacare Will Only Make Health Care Worse: Mayo Drops Medicare," *The Heritage Foundation*, January 4, 2010, http://blog.heritage.org/2010/01/04/obamacare-will-only-make-health-care-worse-mayo-drops-medicare/.

10. *2009 Annual Report of the Boards of Trustees of the Federal Hospital Insurance and Federal Supplementary Medical Insurance Trust Funds*, May 12, 2009, http://www.cms.hhs.gov/reports/trustfunds/downloads/tr2009.pdf.

11. Richard V. Burkhauser, Sean Lyons, and Kosali Simon, *An Offer You Can't Refuse: Estimating the Coverage Effects of the 2010 Affordable Care Act*, Employment Policies Institute, http://epionline.org/downloads/110715_EPI_AnOfferYouCantRefuse_PolicyBrief_Final.pdf.

12. Kathryn Nix, "White House Shirks Responsibility to Address Medicare Insolvency," *The Heritage Foundation*, March 10, 2011, http://blog.heritage.org/2011/03/10/white-house-shirks-responsibility-to-address-medicare-insolvency/.

13. Robert Moffit, "Medicare Provider Cuts Don't Equal Medicare Reform," *The Heritage Foundation*, January 19, 2011, http://www.heritage.org/research/reports/2011/01/obamacare-and-medicare-provider-cuts-jeopardizing-seniors-access.

14. Kelli B. Grant and Sarah Morgan, "13 Simple Ways to Lower Your Electric Bill," *Smart Money*, July 7, 2010, http://www.smartmoney.com/spend/family-money/13-simple-ways-to-lower-your-electric-bill-22933/.

15. Charles W. Bryant, "How Living Off-the-Grid Works," *HowStuffWorks*, January 1, 2012, http://science.howstuffworks.com/environmental/green-science/living-off-the-grid.htm.

16. Rex A. Ewing, "The Real Cost of Going Off-grid," *Countryside & Small Stock Journal*, January 1, 2012, http://www.countrysidemag.com/issues/94/94-2/the_real_cost_of_going_off-grid.html.

17. Charles W. Bryant, "Water and Sewer Off Grid," *HowStuffWorks*, January 1, 2012, http://science.howstuffworks.com/environmental/green-science/living-off-the-grid2.htm.

18. "Septic System Price," *Septic Tank Systems, Portable Washing Machine, Clothes Dryer, The Laundry Alternative Inc*, January 1, 2012, http://www.laundry-alternative.com/septic_system_price.htm.

19. David Goldman, "These Data Miners Know Everything about You," *CNNMoney*, January 1, 2012, http://money.cnn.com/galleries/2010/technology/1012/gallery.data_miners/.

20. Emily Steel, "Using Credit Cards to Target Web Ads," *Wall Street Journal*, October 25, 2011, http://online.wsj.com/article/SB10001424052970204002304576627030651339352.html.

Conclusion

1. "Historical Debt Outstanding—Annual 2000–2010," *TreasuryDirect*, February 22, 2012, http://www.treasurydirect.gov/govt/reports/pd/histdebt/histdebt_histo5.htm.

2. Thomas B. Edsall, "Debt Splits the Left," *Campaign Stops, New York Times*, February 5, 2012, http://campaignstops.blogs.nytimes.com/2012/02/05/debt-splits-the-left/.

3. "U.S. Debt Reaches 100 Percent of Country's GDP," *FOX News*, August 4, 2011, http://www.foxnews.com/politics/2011/08/04/us-debt-reaches-100-percent-countrys-gdp/.

4. Veronique De Rugy, "How Much of Federal Spending Is Borrowed for Every Dollar?" *Mercatus Center, George Mason University*, July 11, 2011, http://mercatus.org/publication/how-much-federal-spending-borrowed-every-dollar.

5. Emily Brandon, "What Social Security's Underfunding Means for Your Retirement," *US News and World Report*, May 13, 2009, http://money.usnews.com/money/retirement/articles/2009/05/13/what-social-securitys-underfunding-means-for-your-retirement.

About the Author

David Voda is a writer, businessman, and investor currently living in Boulder, Colorado.

He has written on business topics for both the *Los Angeles Times* and the *New York Times*, was a Realtor in Palm Springs, California, and buys and sells real estate for his own account. He was a principal in Yes Yes Productions, which produced the award-winning feature, "The Secretary."

Most recently, he was producer of PJTV's business and economics show, *Front Page*.

Index